Race
Capitalism
Justice

*Dedicated to Cedric J. Robinson (1940–2016),
pioneering scholar of racial justice*

Editors Deborah Chasman, Joshua Cohen

Managing Editor Adam McGee

Associate Web and Production Editor Avni Majithia-Sejpal

Associate Editor Matt Lord

Poetry Editors Timothy Donnelly, BK Fischer, Stefania Heim

Fiction Editor Junot Díaz

Editorial Assistants Spencer Ruchti, Andrea Sandell

Poetry Readers Andy Nicole Bowers, William Brewer, Ally Covino, Julie Kantor, Becca Liu, Nick Narbutas, Diana Khoi Nguyen, Charlotte Lieberman, Eleanor Sarasohn, Sean Zhuraw

Publisher Louisa Daniels Kearney

Marketing Manager Anne Boylan

Outreach Kira Brunner Don

Advertising/Sponsorship Christopher Wiss

Finance Manager Anthony DeMusis

Magazine Distributor Disticor Distribution Services
800-668-7724, info@disticor.com

Printer Quad Graphics

Board of Advisors Swati Mylavarapu & Derek Schrier (co-chairs), Archon Fung, Deborah Fung, Richard M. Locke, Timothy Lyster, Jeff Mayersohn, Jennifer Moses, Scott Nielsen, Martha C. Nussbaum, Robert Pollin, Rob Reich, Hiram Samel, Kim Malone Scott

Graphic Design Zak Jensen

Typefaces Druk and Adobe Caslon Pro

To become a member or subscribe, visit:
bostonreview.net/membership/

For questions about subscriptions, call 877-406-2443 or email custsvc_bostonrv@fulcoinc.com. For advertising questions, call 617-324-1325 or email ads@bostonreview.net.

Boston Review
PO Box 425786, Cambridge, MA 02142
617-324-1360

ISSN: 0734-2306

Authors retain copyright of their own work.
© 2017, Boston Critic, Inc.

Contents

Introduction
Robin D. G. Kelley   5

Triptych
Dwayne Betts   9

To Remake the World:
Slavery, Racial Capitalism, and Justice
Walter Johnson   11

32   **History Matters**
Donna Murch

39   **Abolition as Market Regulation**
Caitlin Rosenthal

44   **The Gong of History; Or, What Is a Human?**
Peter Linebaugh

54   **Theories of Justice**
Roberto Gargarella

59   **Racial Capitalism and the Dark Proletariat**
Peter James Hudson

66   **Reviving the Black Radical Tradition**
Manisha Sinha

72   **Putting Rights in Their Place**
Samuel Moyn

78   **What Slavery Tells Us about Marx**
Stephanie Smallwood

83	When Liberalism Defended Slavery *Andrew Zimmerman*
90	Black Humanity and Black Power *Peniel Joseph*
96	This, Our Second Nadir *N. D. B. Connolly*
105	Racial Capitalism and Human Rights *Walter Johnson*

Lake Michigan, Scene 22
Daniel Borzutzky — 113

Births of a Nation:
Surveying Trumpland with Cedric Robinson
Robin D. G. Kelley — 117

From *Good Stock / Strange Blood*
Dawn Lundy Martin — 139

Further Reading — 141

Contributors — 143

Introduction
Robin D. G. Kelley

CEDRIC J. ROBINSON'S PASSING this summer at the age of seventy-five went virtually unnoticed in the media. Professor emeritus of political science and black studies at the University of California, Santa Barbara, Robinson was one of the most original political theorists of his generation, yet no major U.S. newspaper devoted a single paragraph to his memory. Although he deliberately avoided the pitfalls of intellectual celebrity, his influence was greater than perhaps he may have realized. Today's insurgent black movements against state violence and mass incarceration call for an end to "racial capitalism" and see their work as part of a "black radical tradition"—terms associated with Robinson's work.

Born on November 5, 1940, Robinson grew up in a black working-class neighborhood in West Oakland. Educated in public schools, he spent hours in the library absorbing everything from Greek philosophy and world history to literature. Soft-spoken but never "quiet," he attended the University of California, Berkeley, where he majored in anthropology and rose to prominence as a campus activist. He helped bring Malcolm X to campus and protested the Bay of Pigs Invasion, for which he received a one-semester suspension. After graduation in 1963 and a stint in the army, Robinson worked briefly for the Alameda County Probation Department, encountering both a racially biased criminal justice system and fellow employees determined to change it—including his future wife, Elizabeth Peters. By 1967, inspired by the urban rebellions and the antiwar movement, the couple chose to join those determined to change the world, pursuing a life of activism and intellectual work.

In 1974 Robinson earned his doctorate in political theory from Stanford University. His dissertation, "Leadership: A Mythic Paradigm," challenges the conceits of liberal and Marxist theories of political change, arguing that leadership—the idea that effective social action is determined by a leader who is separate from or above the masses of people—and political order are essentially fictions. Contending that "orthodox Western thought was neither universal nor coherent," he ultimately arrives at the conclusion that "the political is an historical . . . illusion." When he submitted a draft of his dissertation in 1971, the faculty was ill-prepared to sign off on a project that questioned the epistemological foundations of the entire discipline. Since no one could reasonably reject a thesis so sound, elegant, and erudite, some members resigned from his committee, citing an inability to understand the work. It took three years and the threat of a lawsuit for his dissertation to be approved, and another six years before it was published as *The Terms of Order: Political Science and the Myth of Leadership* (1980).

Robinson's critique of political order and the authority of leadership anticipated the political currents in contemporary movements such as Occupy Wall Street and Black Lives Matter—movements organized horizontally rather than vertically. His monumental *Black Marxism: The Making of the Black Radical Tradition* (1983) takes Karl Marx to task for failing to comprehend radical movements outside of Europe. He rewrites the history of the West from ancient times to the mid-twentieth century, scrutinizing the idea that Marx's categories of class can be universally applied outside of Europe. Instead he characterized black rebellions as expressions of what he called the "Black Radical Tradition," movements whose objectives and aspirations confounded Western social analysis. Marxism also failed to account for the *racial* character of capitalism. Having written much of the book during a sabbatical year in England, Robinson encountered intellectuals who used the phrase "racial capitalism" to refer to South Africa's economy under apartheid. He developed it from a description of a *specific* system to a way of understanding the *general* history of modern capitalism.

So what did Robinson mean by "racial capitalism"? Building on the work of another forgotten black radical intellectual, sociologist Oliver Cox, Robinson challenged the Marxist idea that capitalism was a revolutionary negation of feudalism. Instead it emerged within the feudal order and flowered in the cultural soil of a Western civilization already thoroughly infused with racialism. Capitalism and racism, in other words, did not break from the old order but rather evolved from it to produce a modern world system of "racial capitalism" dependent on slavery, violence, imperialism, and genocide. Capitalism was "racial" not because of some conspiracy to divide workers or justify slavery and dispossession, but because racialism had already permeated Western feudal society. The first European proletarians were racial subjects (Irish, Jews, Roma or Gypsies, Slavs, etc.) and they were victims of dispossession (enclosure), colonialism, and slavery within Europe. Indeed, Robinson suggested that racialization within Europe was very much a colonial process involving invasion, settlement, expropriation, and racial hierarchy. Insisting that modern European nationalism was completely bound up with racialist myths, he reminds us that the ideology of Herrenvolk (governance by an ethnic majority) that drove German colonization of central Europe and "Slavic" territories "explained the inevitability and the naturalness of the domination of some Europeans by other Europeans." To acknowledge this is not to diminish anti-black racism or African slavery, but to recognize that capitalism was not the great modernizer giving birth to the European proletariat as a universal subject, and the "tendency of European civilization through capitalism was thus not to homogenize but to differentiate—to exaggerate regional, subcultural, and dialectical differences into 'racial' ones."

Black Marxism was largely ignored for two decades, until its return to print in 2000 renewed interest. While Robinson is most known for that book—and its discussion of racial capitalism and the "Black Radical Tradition"—he leaves a vast body of work, notably *Black Movements in America* (1997), *An Anthropology of Marxism* (2001), and *Forgeries of Memory and Meaning: Blacks and the Regimes of Race in American Theater and Film before World War II* (2007).

Robinson was a challenging thinker who understood that the deepest, most profound truths tend to bewilder, breaking with inherited paradigms and "common sense." When asked to define his political commitments, he replied, "There are some realms in which names, nomination, is premature. My only loyalties are to the morally just world; and my happiest and most stunning opportunity for raising hell with corruption and deceit are with other Black people."

In that spirit, the essays that follow apply Robinson's ideas in service of a just world. As Robinson would have hoped, the terrain of their inquiries is wide-ranging, both geographically—from St. Louis to South Africa to South America—and conceptually, as they question a spectrum from orthodox interpretations of Marx to the genealogy of Black Power. Although the contributors often disagree (as Robinson would have expected), they draw from his landmark insights the intellectual and ethical resources required in today's quest for racial justice and the global fight against economic exploitation.

Triptych
Dwayne Betts

But for is always game.
A man can be murdered
twice, but for science,
his body a pool of blood
in Baltimore & Tulsa,
except, it isn't, his body actually
slender against the sunlight just
outside a California prison—a crow
rests on a fence near his car.
Visiting hours long done,
(for man not crow,
one of a murderous many
that flies above this barbed wire)
& the cigarette he smokes
is illegal, here, & but for
the magnetic pull tragedy
has on black women he wouldn't be
here, right now, contemplating
the crimson colored man leaping
into the darkness on his Nikes.
He still says Air Jordans,
because air is important,
adjective swearing to black America's
aim, if not ability, to soar,

a way to outrun statistics
& the lead in the water.
Alas, metaphysics says
you are only you & no one
else, & a black poet says black
love is not one or one thousand
things, & it all may be true,
but for the fact that the man swears
the crow looks at him dead
as if he is already so,
as if while standing there he
has been murdered
by his brother, murdered
by a cop, & bodied
by a prison sentence as flames
from a Newport's burning ash,
illuminate his corpse.

To Remake the World:
Slavery, Racial Capitalism, and Justice
Walter Johnson

IT IS A COMMONPLACE to say that slavery "dehumanized" enslaved people, but to do so is misleading, harmful, and worth resisting.

I hasten to add that there are, of course, plenty of right-minded reasons for adopting the notion of "dehumanization." It is hard to square the idea of millions of people being bought and sold, of systematic sexual violation, natal alienation, forced labor, and starvation with any sort of "humane" behavior: these are the sorts of things that should never be done to human beings. But by terming these actions "inhuman" and suggesting that they either relied upon or accomplished the "dehumanization" of enslaved people, we are participating in a sort of ideological exchange that is no less baleful for being so familiar. We are separating a normative and aspirational notion of humanity from the sorts of exploitation and violence that history suggests may well be *definitive* of human beings: we are separating ourselves from our own histories of perpetration. To say so is not to suggest that there is no difference between the past and the present; it is merely that we should not overwrite the complex determinations of history with simple-minded notions of moral progress.

More important, though, is the ideological work accomplished by holding on to a normative sense of "humanity"—one that can be separated from the "inhuman" actions of so many humans. Historians sometimes argue that some aspects of slavery were so violent, so obscene, so "inhuman" that, in order to live with themselves, the perpetrators had to somehow "dehumanize" their victims. While that "somehow" remains a problem—it is never really specified what combination of unconscious, cultural, and social factors make a "somehow"—I question the assumption that slaveholders had to first "dehumanize" their slaves before they could swing a baby by the feet into a post to silence its cries, or jam the broken handle of a hoe down the throat of a field hand, or refer to their property as "darkies" or "hands" or "wool."

This language of "dehumanization" is misleading because slavery depended upon the human capacities of enslaved people. It depended upon their reproduction. It depended upon their labor. And it depended upon their sentience. Enslaved people could be taught: their intelligence made them valuable. They could be manipulated: their desires could make them pliable. They could be terrorized: their fears could make them controllable. And they could be tortured: beaten, starved, raped, humiliated, degraded. It is these last that are conventionally understood to be the most "inhuman" of slaveholders' actions and those that most "dehumanized" enslaved people. And yet these actions epitomize the failure of this set of terms to capture what was at stake in slaveholding violence: the extent to which slaveholders depended upon violated slaves to bear witness, to provide satisfaction, to provide a living, human register of slaveholders' power.

More than misleading, however, the belief that enslavement "dehumanized" enslaved people is harmful; it indelibly and categorically alters those with whom it supposedly sympathizes. *Dehumanization* suggests an alienation of enslaved people from their humanity. Who is the judge of when a person has suffered so much or been objectified so fundamentally that the person's humanity has been lost? How does the person regain that humanity? Can it even be regained? And who decides when it has been regained? The explicitly paternalist character of these questions suggests that the "dehumanization" of enslaved people is locked in an inextricable embrace with the very history of racial abjection it ostensibly confronts. All this while implicitly asserting the unimpeachable rectitude and "humanity" of latter-day observers.

IT COULD BE ARGUED that my interpretation of the word "dehumanized" is grammatically fundamentalist and intellectually obtuse, that the point of saying that slavery "dehumanized" enslaved people is to draw attention to the immoral actions of *slaveholders—their* inhumanity—rather than to make a claim about the abjection of enslaved people. I would respond by citing Philip Morgan's *Slave Counterpoint*, a prizewinning history of slavery in eighteenth-century North America. In the introduction, Morgan emphasizes that African American slaves "strove . . . to preserve their humanity."

Even as many historians explicitly and insistently vindicate the humanity of enslaved people, they also implicitly and unwittingly suggest that the case for enslaved humanity is in need of being proven again and again. By framing their "discovery" of the enduring humanity of enslaved people as a defining feature of their work, by casting their work as proof of black humanity—as if this were a question that should even be posed—historians ironically render black humanity intellectually probationary. Efforts to separate "human" from "inhuman" and "dehumanized" thus create an unanticipated set of intellectual and ethical overflows.

Elsewhere in the same introduction, Morgan writes:

> Wherever and whenever masters, whether implicitly or explicitly, recognized the independent will and volition of their slaves, they acknowledged the humanity of their bondpeople. Extracting this admission was, in fact, a form of slave resistance, because slaves thereby opposed the dehumanization inherent in their status.

I want to emphasize that I am not quoting these sentences because they are exceptionally imperceptive. I quote them because they are emblematic: by counterpoising an emphasis on "independent will and volition" against the possibility of "dehumanization," they crystallize a set of intellectual impulses and ethical premises that undergirds much of the scholarship on slavery. They frame their account of humanity as an aspect of the problem of freedom, and freedom of a very particular sort: the freedom to make choices and take intended actions—in other words, the bourgeois freedoms of classical liberalism. In so doing, they point to the peculiar complications that result from positioning the history of slavery at the juncture of the terms "human" and "rights."

Several problems flow from the assumption that every history of slavery is peopled by liberal subjects striving to be emancipated into the political condition of the twenty-first-century Western bourgeoisie. From a historiographic perspective, we could say that this perspective alienates enslaved people from the historical parameters and cultural determinants of their own actions. It takes their actions—from singing a spiritual to breaking a tool to fomenting a revolution to having a good idea about how to run a better sluiceway—and collapses them down to a single anachronistic and essentially liberal moral: enslaved people's "agency" proved their humanity.

I am less interested here in the historiographic implications of this line of reasoning than I am in its ethical dimensions. The tension between the specific actions and idioms of enslaved life and the broadly comparative categories of "independent will and volition," "agency," and "humanity" seem analogically—and, indeed, historically and ethically—related to the tension that Karl Marx noted between the historical and material inequalities of nineteenth-century society and the abstract equality of rights-based human emancipation, of which he was critical. In his essay "On the Jewish Question," Marx wrote that the political citizen was "an imaginary member of an imaginary universality." For Marx the material salients of human existence—"distinctions of birth, social rank, education, occupation"—continued to guide and determine the course of history, even as the inauguration of a new sort of history, the history of political equality, was announced to the world. In a passage that captures both the terrific promises and bounded limits of a rights-based notion of human emancipation, Marx wrote:

> Political emancipation is, of course, a big step forward. True, it is not the final form of human emancipation, but it is the final form of human emancipation within the hitherto existing world order. It goes without saying that we are speaking here of [something greater than that] real, practical emancipation.

It is through Marx's appreciation for and critique of citizenship—and, by extension, of the rights-based notion of the human being at the heart of the historiography of slavery—that I want to turn more directly to the question of human rights.

A GOOD DEAL OF recent scholarship has emphasized the importance of both vernacular and institutional antislavery to the intellectual history of human rights. Samuel Moyn's influential account of the history of human rights, however, departs from this timeline to argue for a much later set of historical benchmarks. It was not until well into the twentieth century, Moyn argues, that the idea of "a new world" emerged, "in which the dignity of each individual will enjoy secure international protection." While many other scholars are critical of the way that Moyn's timeline sets the history of slavery and antislavery to the side of the history of human rights, I think Moyn is not without reason. The version of human rights that dominates contemporary super-sovereign rights claims, I would suggest, is not significantly inflected by the history of slavery, although it would be better if it were.

Our current understanding of universal human rights has its origin in a particular historical experience: that of Europe in the twentieth century. Human-rights thinking has emphasized the universal rights of democratic self-determination, freedom of conscience and expression, protection from political violence and, above all, the anathematization of genocide. Paraphrasing Marx, I think it is fair to say that the emergence of a global movement in support of human rights is the summary accomplishment of "the hitherto existing world order." It is not, however—nor in my view should it be—"the final form of human emancipation" or of what a just world should look like. In Moyn's view, in fact, human-rights thinking has provided the intellectual architecture for a sort of liberal neo-imperialism, the justifying terms of continuing European and American intervention in the affairs of former colonies.

There is a quite different genealogy for discussions of human freedom—this one rooted in the experience of slavery rather than the question of the humanity of slaves. The Movement for Black Lives proposal, "A Vision for Black Lives," insists on a relationship between the history of slavery and contemporary struggles for social justice. At the heart of the proposal is a call for "reparations for the historic and continuing harms of colonialism and slavery." Indeed, the ambient as well as the activist discussion of justice in the United States today is inseparable from the history of slavery.

With this in mind, we might return to the question of "human emancipation"—this time with the purpose of essaying a definition of justice that is rooted in the history of slavery and goes beyond liberal human rights. Through this route, we can arrive at a history of the global political economy that is attentive to what, following Cedric Robinson, I term racial capitalism.

In *Black Marxism* (1983), Robinson argues that the historical developments of capitalism and racism were inseparable. Engaging with black nationalism and orthodox Marxism, he argues that the path toward the just and the good cannot be found in the "authoritarian" pronouncements of uninflected Marxism, with its single route to revolution, nor in the historical "simplications" of black nationalism, which threatens to replicate white-dominated institutions but with black people in charge. Instead the path to justice is located in the black radical tradition: in the democratic practices and revolutionary thought of black people living under conditions of racial capitalism.

Black Marxism begins with a history of slavery in medieval Europe, in part to demonstrate the historically contingent character of the relationship between slavery and blackness. It then turns to the early modern period and the European enslavement of Africans. In the era of the Atlantic slave trade, new notions of difference—absolute, racial notions of difference—were used to define, describe, and justify the political economy of slavery.

For Robinson, W. E. B. Du Bois was the preeminent historian of the ways that racism had defined the history of capitalism and interrupted the universalist pretensions of Marxist orthodoxy. In a 1920 essay entitled "The Souls of White Folk," Du Bois suggests that both economic exploitation and domination justified by imagined difference have histories "as old as mankind." But their combination in European imperialism—the "discovery of personal whiteness" by those who claimed title to the world and the concomitant designation of the world's dark peoples as "beasts of burden"—is recent, a product of the slave trade. Gone in Du Bois are the orthodox markers that serve to keep the history of slavery separate from the history of capitalism. In their place Du Bois proposes a new milestone, the emergence of a sort of capitalism that relies upon the elaboration, reproduction, and exploitation of notions of racial difference: a global capitalism concomitant with the invention of what Robinson termed "the universal Negro." In short: racial capitalism.

In *Black Reconstruction in America*, published fifteen years later, Du Bois roots his account of racial capitalism in the history of slavery in the United States. "The giant forces of water and of steam were harnessed to do the world's work, and the black workers of America bent at the bottom of a growing pyramid of commerce and industry; and they not only could not be spared, if this new economic organization was to expand, but rather they became the cause of new political demands and alignments, of new dreams of power and visions of empire," he writes in the book's first pages.

> Black labor became the foundation stone not only of the Southern social structure, but of Northern manufacture and commerce, of the English factory system, of European commerce, of buying and selling on a worldwide scale; new cities were built on the results of black labor, and a new labor problem, involving all white labor, arose in both Europe and America.

In a few sentences, Du Bois scuttles the orthodox separation of slavery and capitalism. He names his history of American slavery "The Black Worker"—a subject, at once, of capital and of white supremacy. This, Robinson writes, was "the beginning of the transformation of the historiography of American Civilization—the naming of things."

Rather than following Adam Smith or Karl Marx, each of whom viewed slavery as a residual form in the world of emergent capitalism, Du Bois treats the plantations of Mississippi, the counting houses of Manhattan, and the mills of Manchester as differentiated but concomitant components of a single system. Many scholars have expressed a fear that terming both what happened in Mississippi and what happened in Manchester "capitalism" will make it impossible to see the trees for the forest—"obscuring," in the words of James Oakes, "fundamental differences between economies based on enslaved [and] free labor." But there is no obvious reason that should be the case. Arguing that the history of (racial) capitalism began with the slave trade rather than the factory system does not necessarily pose any greater threat to historical and analytical precision than arguing that both Harriet Tubman and John C. Calhoun were human beings.

Indeed, Du Bois draws attention to the very differences that Oakes worries will be elided. He simply sees the production of these differences as an aspect of the history he is trying to understand, rather than as an inevitable answer to which any historical account must aspire. The history of white working-class struggle, for example, cannot be understood separate from the privileges of whiteness, to which the white working classes of Britain and the United States laid claim in their demands for equal political rights. And it was the ever-expanding frontier of imperialism and racial capitalism that pacified the white working class with the threat of replacement and promise of a share of the spoils. The history of racial capitalism, it must be emphasized, is a history of wages as well as whips, of factories as well as plantations, of whiteness as well as blackness, of "freedom" as well as slavery.

Critically, there is nothing static or simple about this formulation. Du Bois does not argue that all whites benefit from capitalism while all blacks do not. But nor does he argue that blacks and whites are "workers" in the same way. He suggests instead a subtle and dynamic relationship between capitalist exploitation and white supremacy. Likewise, he insists on a coeval and dialectical relationship between metropole and colony: even as the economic spaces of the Global South were reconfigured in relation to northern capital, metropolitan class relationships were reconfigured around ideas of freedom and entitlement that emerged from imperialism and slavery.

Du Bois's invocation of the "wages of whiteness" can best be understood in the context of a global economy that entwined Mississippi, Manhattan, and Manchester together in a white-supremacist system of differential rights and entitlements. Under the dominion of cotton, metropolitan wage workers came to understand themselves as white and to measure their entitlement in terms of slavery and empire: as natural and just when they shared in the spoils; as insupportable and impious when they did not.

Far from obscuring the differences between the social relations of production in the various regions of the world, *Black Reconstruction* provides an account of their historical interconnection, their racial predication, and their functional differentiation. "The abolition of American slavery," Du Bois writes, "started the transportation of capital from white to black countries where slavery prevailed . . . and precipitated the modern economic degradation of the white farmer, while it put into the hands of the owners of the machine such a monopoly of raw material that their dominion of white labor was more and more complete." The end of U.S. slavery, according to Du Bois, marked not the liberation of the independent forces of capitalism and freedom from their archaic interconnection with slavery, but the global generalization of the racial and imperial vision of the "empire of cotton." The history of racial capitalism is a history of the interconnected process by which economic, geographic, and racial differences were seeded, took root, and finally grew up to such an extent that they obscured efforts to search out their common origin: a history, at once, of integrative connection and divisive particularization.

The fullest expression of Du Bois's account of global racial capitalism is in *The World and Africa* (1946). There he describes the process by which "slavery and the slave trade became transformed into anti-slavery and colonialism, and all with the same determination and demand to increase profit an investment." Although this meant that terms of European stewardship were transformed, even at times inverted, the racial pattern of extraction and exploitation nonetheless continued unabated.

> It all became a characteristic drama of capitalist exploitation, where the right hand knew nothing of what the left hand did, yet rhymed its grip with uncanny timeliness; where the investor neither knew, nor inquired, nor greatly cared about the sources of his profits; where the enslaved or dead or half-paid worker never saw nor dreamed of the value of his work (now owned by others); where neither the society darling nor the great artist saw the blood on the piano keys; where the clubman, boasting of great game hunting, heard above the click of his smooth, lovely, resilient billiard balls no echo of the wild shrieks of pain from kindly, half-human beasts as fifty to seventy-five thousand each year were slaughtered in cold, cruel, lingering horror of living death; sending their teeth to adorn civilization on the bowed heads and chained feet of thirty thousand black slaves, leaving behind more than a hundred thousand corpses in broken, flaming homes.

As much as anything, this is an account of the spatial aspect of racial capitalism. It emphasizes both the intimate, violent proximities and the material and cognitive distances of region, race, and scale (global and imperial, intimate and proximate). Du Bois's account is particularly interested in the material culture of racial capital, of how the suffering of dead elephants and enslaved Africans was reassembled elsewhere as sensory pleasures for the parlors and pool halls of imperial London. It is an environmental history of the resource-extracting, race-differentiating, world-wasting race to the end of time. Uncannily, the most ambitious and perceptive examples of the "new history of capitalism" turn out to have been written over seventy years ago.

IMPLICIT IN THE INSIGHT of racial capitalism is the claim that something fundamental and racial (or, more precisely, rac*ist*) is elided by the conventional understanding of capitalism's origins. Critics of the traditional account must show what is gained by thinking outward from the history of slavery to an overarching idea of racial capitalism. A history of capitalism framed by categories derived from analysis of the mills of Manchester might have made sense in the era of the miners' strike in Great Britain or of George Meany and the AFL-CIO in the United States (although the murder of Vincent Chin, among countless other examples, suggests otherwise). The history of American slavery, however, seems a more apt starting point for the analysis of a world characterized by the global division of labor, the resurgence of slavery as mode of production, the emergence of personal services (and pornography) as leading sectors of the economy, and the effulgence of nativism and white nationalism as fundamental features of white working-class ideology. History has moved on, and in so doing it has reshuffled its own past.

Indeed, the history of capitalism makes no sense separate from the history of the slave trade and its aftermath. There was no such thing as capitalism without slavery: the history of Manchester never happened without the history of Mississippi. In *Capitalism and Slavery* (1944), Eric Williams gives a detailed account of the supersession of British colonial interests by manufacturing ones and the replacement of cotton with sugar as the foundation of capitalist development. Williams argues that Great Britain freed its slaves, but did not free itself from slavery. British capitalists simply outsourced the production of the raw material upon which they principally depended to the United States. During the antebellum period, 85 percent of the cotton produced in the United States was exported to Great Britain. During the same period, 85 percent of the cotton manufactured in Great Britain was imported in raw form from the United States. Raw cotton was thus the largest single export of the United States and the largest single import of Great Britain.

Trying to abstract the social relations of production that characterized British (or American) cotton mills from the rest of the economy that gave them life—and then identifying this as the paradigmatic example of "capitalism"—quite simply does not make sense. "Would Great Britain have industrialized without slavery, though perhaps at a different pace or in a different way?" James Oakes has recently written. What is being proposed is an adventitious, ahistorical definition of capitalism—a thing which might have happened even though it actually did not—that serves no purpose except to preserve, at whatever cost, the analytical precedence of Europe over Africa, the factory over the field, and the white working class over black slaves. Capitalism counterfactually emancipated from slavery. That is not social science; it is science fiction.

Rather than asking over and over what Marx said about slavery, we should follow Robinson in asking what slavery says about Marx. We should use the history of slavery as the source rather than the subject of knowledge. Let us begin with the most basic distinction in political economy: the distinction between capital and labor. Enslaved people were both. Their double economic aspect could not be separated and graphed on the axes of a Cartesian grid; their interests could not be balanced against one another or subordinated to one another in an effort to secure social order. They were both.

And so, too, were their children: racial capitalism swung on a reproductive hinge. The entire "pyramid" of the Atlantic economy of the nineteenth century (the economy that has been treated as the paradigmatic example of capitalism) was founded upon the capacity of enslaved women's bodies: upon their ability to reproduce capital. As Deborah Gray White points out, sexual violation, reproductive invigilation, and natal alienation were elementary aspects of slavery, and thus of racial capitalism. The alternative, of course, was the slave trade. As the slaveholder J. D. B. DeBow stated in his 1858 argument for reopening the Atlantic slave trade to the United States (which had been outlawed in 1808), it was either that or "await with folded arms the coming of population and of labor which will be the result of natural increase." A commercial mode of social reproduction would make black women disposable.

The political economy of the nineteenth century was founded on these basic facts. Every year the cotton merchants of Great Britain made tremendous advances to the cotton planters of the South. The planters used the credit to purchase seeds and tools and slaves and the food to feed them, and they planned to use those slaves to plant and pick and pack and ship the cotton that would cover the money that had been advanced to them, and then some. As pro-slavery political economist Thomas Kettel wrote in 1860:

> The agriculturalists, who create the real wealth of the country, are not in daily receipt of money. Their produce is ready but once a year, whereas they buy supplies [on credit] year round. . . . The whole banking system of the country is based primarily on this bill movement against produce.

In case the cotton proved too scant or poor to cover the amount that had been advanced against its eventual sale, or in case the cotton market dipped in the time between when an advance was made and the time the crop came in, cotton merchants required some sort of security from the planters to whom they loaned money. That security was the value of the enslaved. Therefore, given that enslaved people were the collateral upon which the entire system depended, it seems absurd to persist in asking whether the political economy of slavery was or was not "capitalist." *Enslaved people were the capital.* Their value in 1860 was equal to all of the capital invested in American railroads, manufacturing, and agricultural land combined.

It is important to add that the land tells a different part of the story, one that resounds with Du Bois's emphasis on empire alongside enslavement as the primary categories of capitalist accumulation. The land that enslaved people planted in cotton and which their owners posted as collateral was Native American land: it had been expropriated from the Creek, the Cherokee, the Choctaw, the Chickasaw, and the Seminole. Indeed, if one traces the legal history of private property in the United States back, trying to find a legal foundation for determining why (legally rather than morally speaking) we own what we think we own, at the bottom lies the decision of the United States Supreme Court in the case of *Johnson v. McIntosh* (1823). At stake in the case was the question of whether white settlers could purchase land directly from native inhabitants, and the answer of the Supreme Court was "no." Native American lands, the court ruled, must be passed through the public domain of the United States before being converted into the private property of white inhabitants. In other words, the foundation of the law of property in the United States combines, at once, the imperial assertion of U.S. sovereignty and the identification of that project with continental racial governance.

The racial capitalism of the nineteenth century was founded upon the racialization and instrumentalization, the commodification and securitization, the expropriation and forcible transportation, the sexual violation and reproductive alienation of Africans and Native Americans. It is here we must begin to reimagine the categories against which we stretch the past into historical meaning, to follow the lead of those who self-consciously work in the tradition of Du Bois and Robinson: scholars such as Ruth Wilson Gilmore, Adam Green, Cheryl Harris, Peter Hudson, Robin D. G. Kelley, George Lipsitz, Lisa Lowe, Gary Okihiro, Nell Irvin Painter, David Roediger, Alexander Saxton, and Stephanie Smallwood. And no longer should the "capitalism–slavery debate" proceed without a full and forthright acknowledgement of and engagement with the pioneering work and enduring insights of W. E. B. Du Bois, C. L. R. James, Eric Williams, Walter Rodney, Angela Davis, and Cedric Robinson.

THESE CONSIDERATIONS SHED LIGHT on the relationship between slavery and contemporary ideas of justice. Tragically, the history of slavery is increasingly being written without enslaved people. By this, I mean that a field formerly defined by the dissident, bottom-up methodology of black studies and social history is increasingly dominated by work that does not ask questions about the experiences, ideas, or history of the enslaved (even while it teaches us many new things about slaveholders and their business partners). Let me be clear: it is not only nonsensical but also unethical to continue asking whether slavery was capitalist without asking what that meant to enslaved people—to investigate what Du Bois termed "the philosophy of life and action which slavery bred in the souls of black folk."

What does the history of the enslaved tell us about the question of rights? I began by suggesting that much of the scholarship on slavery has relied upon a pat liberal notion of human rights as its moral paradigm —despite the clear contradiction between the universalization of a bourgeois liberal actor and the legal and experiential realities of slavery. The culturally dominant notion of human rights is not only unreflective of the history of slavery; it is unresponsive to the specific patterns of injustice that follow from the history of slavery. In its place, I suggest the possibility of using the history of slavery as a standpoint from which to rethink our idea of justice. What is left is to delineate the usefulness of this history to an account of justice.

There are six principal virtues of an account of justice rooted in the history of slavery and racial capitalism:

First, it mounts its critique of modern injustice from the standpoint of Africa and "the Global South," rather than from Europe and "the Global North."

Second, it focuses on the extraction and distribution of resources between classes and areas of the world: on the relationship of African American history to Native American history, for example, or on the relationship of either or both of those to the history of the white workers (and merchants and bankers) in the financial and manufacturing centers of the United States and Europe. So doing, it proposes the generalization of an account of historical wrong based in the experiences of the dark and dispossessed rather than in those of the metropolitan bourgeoisie.

Third, it emphasizes the ways in which present distributions of privilege and abjection are related to past patterns. It opens a pathway along which historically deep notions of restorative justice and reparations, rather than a synchronic focus on "rights," might be seen as the only adequate form of redress.

Fourth, it insists upon a sense of justice attentive to questions of gender and sexuality, on the ways that reproductive invigilation and natal alienation—the subordination of the social reproduction of one group of people to the purposes of another—were core features of the human wrongs of slavery.

Fifth, it asserts a direct relationship between—and indeed, the functional sameness of—what are conventionally separated as the politics of "race" and "class." It correlates both the entitlement and vulnerability of the white working class with the subjection of the "dark proletariat," and connects the insistent racialization of the global working class to the operations of capital.

Sixth, it suggests the possibility of relating a critique of the instrumentalization of human beings through slavery to the instrumentalization of nature in capitalist forms of extraction. Over and against many recent efforts which assert that a forthright treatment of global environmental history requires the elevation of the categories of the "human" and the "Anthropocene" over and against other historical categories—principally those of race, class, gender, and colonialism—it insists upon the intimate and dialectical relationship between domination and dominion.

In *The Suppression of the African Slave Trade to the United States of America* (1896), an extended description of the various heartless and cynical prevarications through which the United States evaded the suppression of the Atlantic slave trade, Du Bois makes an argument about the character of historical time. There are, in his view, moments that are propitious for change, moments when it is possible—with courageous and concerted action—to remake the world in its own better image. The cost, for Du Bois, of missing those moments can only be reckoned in the blood of the subsequent generations, who pay the price for their forebears' failures. Perhaps we should heed his warning.

History Matters
Donna Murch

WALTER JOHNSON ARGUES AGAINST a triumphalist narrative of liberal human rights that elides the bloody past of racial slavery and land expropriation in the United States. Taking to task eminent slavery scholars Philip Morgan and James Oakes and a voluminous literature on human rights, Johnson argues that "we are separating a normative and aspirational notion of humanity from the sorts of exploitation and violence" that may well typify human behavior itself, "separating ourselves from our own histories of perpetration."

By invoking the black radical intellectual tradition of W. E. B. Du Bois, Eric Williams, Walter Rodney, C. L. R. James, Angela Davis, and Cedric Robinson, Johnson counters the subterranean creep into historical scholarship of liberal notions of justice. In its place Johnson proposes an alternate genealogy in which the original sins of indigenous land seizure and the Atlantic slave trade served as the genesis of global capitalism. Calling on historians to revisit and expand their understanding of primitive accumulation, Johnson explains, "Rather than asking over and over what Marx said about slavery, we should follow Robinson in asking what slavery says about Marx." He laments that slavery remains insufficiently integrated into the history of capitalism, just as the historical experience of enslaved people themselves has become marginalized in some of the most elite academic circles.

Since the Great Compromise of 1877, the history of slavery, emancipation, and Reconstruction has been one of the most deeply politicized arenas of American history. For nearly a century, a white supremacist view of the "peculiar institution" dominated university studies, with slavery represented neither as capitalist nor as harmful to the enslaved. Instead African enslavement was understood as either the continuation of a feudal order awaiting the modernizing tide of market forces or as a civilizing mission that delivered the backward peoples of Africa into enlightened modernity. Du Bois's *The Suppression of the African Slave Trade to the United States of America* (1896) and *Black Reconstruction in America* (1935), as well as Trinidadian scholar Eric Williams's *Capitalism and Slavery* (1944), offered dissenting perspectives, but racial segregation in the university limited their sphere of influence.

With the massive social upheaval of the post–World War II African American freedom struggle, benign accounts of chattel slavery became increasingly obsolete. Buttressed by the burgeoning civil rights movement's battles against legal segregation in the South and racial inequalities in housing, education, and jobs in the North, a subsequent generation of postwar slavery historiography viewed U.S. slavery from the "bottom up." The desire to understand the interplay of capitalist forces in chattel slavery and the slave trade accompanied a search to document the experiences of enslaved peoples themselves. These two schools of thought did not always agree, but taken together they represented an important shift towards the radical social history of the 1960s and '70s.

Walter Johnson now offers a crucial critique of a new wave of historiographic "common sense" that has again shifted back toward an elite focus on "slaveholders and their business partners," often to the exclusion of the enslaved. Strikingly, this turn among a select group of historians of capitalism and slavery takes place during a time of extreme state violence against people of color, from Ferguson to Standing Rock; two of the longest imperial wars in history, waged in Iraq and Afghanistan; neoliberal retreat from the welfare state; and the legal evisceration of voting rights' protections. Following Du Bois, Johnson pushes against this scholarship, arguing instead for the "subtle and dynamic relationship between capitalist exploitation and white supremacy." And of course he is not alone in this enterprise: while Johnson takes some of the field's elder statesmen to task, his larger project has been realized by numerous contemporaries, including Jennifer Morgan, Peter Hudson, Stephanie Camp, Stephanie Smallwood, Ed Baptist, Marisa Fuentes, Walter Rucker, Barbara Krauthamer, Rashauna Johnson, Jessica Marie Johnson, Vanessa Holden, and Caleb McDaniel.

Johnson's essay is politically urgent. The framework he offers for understanding racial capitalism matters in and beyond the university, perhaps most immediately for our collective national memory during Donald Trump's presidency. While Johnson focuses on how professional historians study and understand chattel slavery and Native land expropriation, his essay avails us of tools to analyze later periods of American history, including the country's steady march to the right over the past half-century.

Johnson insists on placing the United States in a broader global frame that includes histories of imperial conquest levied at the expense of the "dark and dispossessed." His point helps explain why so many liberal (and left) intellectuals in the United States look longingly toward Europe. The sense is that if we could just stop focusing on race by grounding ourselves in Enlightenment universals, we could begin to build a European-style social democracy. Too often the points of comparison for this political project are wealthy Western nation-states such as England, Germany, and France. But given our history as a settler colony built through a centuries-long process of land seizure and racial slavery, a more apt set of comparisons would include Australia, Brazil, and South Africa. It is telling that South Africa has the most unequal distribution of wealth in the world.

Indeed, the concept of racial capitalism first emerged in the decades before the overthrow of the apartheid state in South Africa. Marxist activists and radical members of the Black Consciousness movement developed this framework to understand the resilience of apartheid rule. First applied to the Americas in Cedric Robinson's groundbreaking *Black Marxism* (1983), the conceptual groundwork for racial capitalism emerged out of collaborative political work in South Africa to understand why portions of the country's white working class and black middle class supported a racial state presided over by a white capitalist class. In his forthcoming book, *Neoliberal Apartheid*, sociologist Andy Clarno argues that at the core of racial capitalism is "the recognition that racialization and capital accumulation are mutually constitutive processes that combine in dynamic, context-specific formations." The processes of dispossession, coerced labor, sexual violence, and forced reproduction, documented in Deborah Gray White's *Ar'n't I a Woman?* (1999), remind us that race, class, gender, and sexuality can never be separated or understood in isolation from one another.

These historical questions are not mere matters of disinterested contemplation. We are living in a time of misplaced anger and conscious forgetting, in which critics from venues as diverse as the *New York Times* and *Jacobin* have railed against a vague and capacious thing that they dismiss as "identity politics." This fungible category seems to mean everything from the rights-based logic manifest in the Civil Rights and Voting Rights Acts of the mid-1960s to the contemporary insistence on campus "safe spaces" for college students. It has been held responsible for the defeat of the Democratic Party and for the elevation of a crude real estate tycoon turned media celebrity to America's forty-fifth presidency.

What is omitted from this analysis is as telling as what is included. Foremost is the role of voter disfranchisement in the 2016 election. Currently nearly six million people are disfranchised because of felony convictions, with one in thirteen African Americans unable to participate in the democratic process. The critique of a nebulous identity politics, which often targets precisely the populations placed in the cross hairs of the incoming administration, ignores the explicit racialization of economic issues that catapulted Trump into office. Each of his recurrent campaign promises—to tear up trade agreements, build a wall along the Mexican border, and "drain the swamp" of campaign finance—corresponded to economic expectations of white voters across class lines. Trump mobilized feelings of resentment to target working populations that are poorer per capita than his white supporters, with Latino families possessing one-tenth the wealth of the average white family, and black families possessing one-thirteenth. Trump made this agenda ever more explicit by choosing racists and billionaires for his cabinet. Among other appointees, Trump selected an avowed white nationalist, Stephen Bannon, and Michael Flynn, who advocates a global war on the Islamic State.

We seem destined to relive many of the racial legacies of our founding. Trump's promise or threat—depending on your subject position—to "Make America Great Again" demonstrates this tendency, as does the recourse to mythic narratives of the American past to explain his success. Among the most improbable of Trump's media-driven misrepresentations has been his transformation into a personification of white working-class revolt, which helped mobilize the economic anxieties and fears of a population that feels neglected by the Washington establishment. Downward mobility, loss of wealth, and economic instability are unquestionably affecting all residents of the United States. But the singular focus on whites as embodying a deracialized set of "class-based interests" must be understood as an inheritance of slavery, Jim Crow, and the long racialization of state practices, such that whiteness is often both invisible and normative in matters of citizenship.

Political scientist Mark Lilla, whose *New York Times* op-ed went viral after the election, argues that the Democratic Party should embrace the unifying visions of Ronald Reagan and Bill Clinton. He praises Clinton, in particular, for seizing control of the party from its "identity conscious wing" and "appealing to Americans as Americans and emphasizing the issues that affect a vast majority of them." Strikingly, Lilla is silent on the topic of Clinton's signing of the North American Free Trade Agreement (NAFTA) and on his elimination of the Glass-Steagall Act, which many have argued paved the way for the 2008 financial crisis. Instead, drawing on the potent racial trope of Nixon's silent majority, Lilla laments, "The media's newfound, almost anthropological, interest in the angry white male reveals as much about the state of our liberalism as it does about this much maligned, and previously ignored, figure." In a perverse twist, Lilla singles out the Ku Klux Klan as America's first identity-based movement. This remarkable exercise in denial and forgetting collapses the distinction between the struggle of African Americans to realize their rights and a vigilante organization aimed at maintaining white rule.

As Lilla and others have made clear, post-racialism haunts American popular media as well as the university. The framework of racial capitalism offers a powerful alternative that allows us to talk about the urgency of redistributive justice. Only a reckoning with our *longue durée* history—one that acknowledges capitalism's genesis in Atlantic slavery—can help us to understand why race, class, gender, and sexuality cannot be productively disentangled in our present struggles for a just society. As Stuart Hall aphorized, race is the modality through which class is lived. Likewise, Johnson reminds us of the importance of black radical thought and the anti-colonial left to how we understand our shared history as well as our present moment.

Abolition as Market Regulation
Caitlin Rosenthal

WHAT LANGUAGE SHOULD WE use when we talk about slavery? Walter Johnson takes historians to task for using the word "dehumanize." While I am skeptical about the dangers of the word itself, I strongly agree that the discourse about slavery should not be artificially separated from conversations about modern capitalism. How does the history of slavery look if we make more use of the language of capitalism?

One place to begin is to describe the abolition of slavery not as a human-rights measure but as a form of market regulation. In the abstract, this shift makes sense: abolition not only stripped slaveholders of their property, it also restricted property rights. It prevented men and women from being sold (or selling themselves) into bondage. Abolition also outlawed certain kinds of transactions and, as a regulation of "bonds," it restricted the right to contract.

Framing abolition as market regulation inverts conventional ideas about slavery and capitalism, particularly the assumption that free markets are fundamentally connected to other human freedoms. The shared modifier "free" elides vast differences between free markets and other kinds of freedoms: freedom to move, to speak, to assemble, to love. History suggests that these freedoms can both expand together and move in opposition to one another. In the Atlantic world, "free" trade in goods (and bodies) expanded even as millions of Africans lost control over their lives and labor. The relationship between free markets and other freedoms is not inevitable.

Describing the abolition and amelioration of slavery as "market regulations" has the effect of recasting them as a series of trade deals. Concern for the enslaved played a role, just as concern for workers does in trade deals today. But so did economic growth and stability. Take the 1833 act that abolished slavery in the British Empire. The measure was a carefully negotiated set of compromises that looked out for the interests of the enslavers as well as the enslaved. Only slaves under the age of six were actually liberated. Older slaves were rebound to work during a period of apprenticeship, and planters were paid for their loss of property.

Compensated emancipation was the norm. Across the Atlantic, slaveholders were paid in cash, through a period of labor, or both. Even when slavery ended by war, the "expropriated" owners were sometimes paid for their "losses." After the Haitian Revolution, the former slaves paid reparations to France to compensate their former masters. No one compensated the slaves. Even at moments of emancipation, the enslaved were never seen as the ones who had been expropriated.

If abolition was a form of market regulation, then the economic circumstances of slavery appear as an unfettered marketplace—at least from the perspective of capitalist planters. They could (and did) employ wage laborers. But they could also purchase slaves, uprooting them and relocating them to new geographies and fertile plots of soil. Once they had secured labor, planters could turn to both positive and negative incentives to spur action. None of this had yet been regulated.

The enslaved did not enjoy the same economic opportunities, but they nonetheless often participated in markets. Though they did not own their own labor, in some places they could aspire to purchase themselves. And they engaged in a wide array of smaller commercial transactions. As recent research by Justene Hill shows, these exchanges usually benefitted masters more than slaves, but unequal access is not unusual in capitalist market spaces. When employers sell goods to their workers, it often increases both their profits and their control over labor.

Just as the word "regulation" offers a fresh perspective on abolition, the words Johnson proposes—"commodification," "securitization," "instrumentalization," and others—can tell us about how slavery functioned on the ground. A range of historians, including Stephanie Smallwood and Daina Ramey Berry, have already put some of this language to use. More terms could be added to the list, some of them used by slaveholders themselves. For example, in my own research on the history of accounting, I examine how planters "appreciated" and "depreciated" slaves and described it in these terms. They tracked the increasing value of enslaved children as they approached adulthood and the declining value of those who ran away, became sick, or simply grew old.

Take the word "commodify." At its most general, it simply means to make marketable. But it also carries a more specific meaning: to transform into a commodity good. That is, something that is graded and measured, and thus fungible and interchangeable. From the perspective of the buyer, any unit of a commodity is identical to any another. One Grade A extra large egg. One bushel of No. 1 spring wheat. One bale of strict good middling cotton.

Planters developed rating scales and categories to do just this with their slaves. They priced them by height and occasionally by weight. They rated them as quarter, half, three-quarter, and full hands (a full "hand" being an able-bodied adult slave who could labor at a high level). This system allowed slaveholders to set a wide variety of human lives equivalent to one another. A gang of enslaved children rated as quarter- and half-hands, for example, could be summed and set equal to a smaller number of men and women of prime age. The process of commodification was not as complete as it was for other "goods"—there were no futures contracts for slaves. But the extent of commodification was remarkable. Before the closing of the Atlantic slave trade, "New Negroes" from Africa were even included in some prices currents right alongside the goods they grew. A 1785 price list, for example, includes a wide range of commodities, many of them grown and produced by enslaved peoples—coffee, tobacco, indigo, rice, and of course sugar, molasses, and rum. At the end of the list is "New Negroes, 30l to 40l cash" or "50l [to] 60l at 6, 9, or 12 months credit."

Of course, even as the language of capital opens up new questions, it too falls short. So much of the vocabulary of modern capitalism is about reducing goods to something simpler than they are in order to adapt them to the market. To be commoditized is to be reduced to a commodity. To be securitized is to be structured into a schedule of payments and a hierarchy of claimants, and thus made ready for sale. To be instrumentalized is to be merely a tool. There is nothing inherently violent in these processes of simplification. But we balk at their application to lives. We are horrified to see men, women, and children subjected to this kind of reduction. It cuts at what it is to be human, then and now.

Ironically, then, applying the language of capital to the circumstances of slavery brings us back to the discarded word: "dehumanization." Johnson eloquently explains how the term can inappropriately frame enslaved humanity in terms of "the bourgeois freedoms of classical liberalism." But, used carefully, the word can trade this academic baggage for a simpler meaning. To speak of dehumanization can be a way of acknowledging what is lost in the language of capital. The Oxford English Dictionary traces the word "dehumanize" to the early nineteenth century and defines it as "to deprive of human character or attributes." "Humanize" is older, dating to at least the early seventeenth century. Among its various meanings we find "to represent in human form." Humanization and dehumanization characterize processes of representation, and they can be used to explore the ways the language of capital pushes toward the commodification, securitization, instrumentalization, and alienation of everything—even lives, if our laws allow it to do so.

The vocabulary of capitalism can help us to see the economic system of Atlantic slavery for what it was: an unfettered wilderness of exchange where even lives were up for sale. And the words we use to write the history of slavery—however imperfectly—can help us to describe the dangers of deregulated capitalism. One of the most basic lessons to be gleaned from the history of slavery is how readily men and women exploit and abuse one another, given the opportunity—how far everyday people will go in pursuit of power, influence, and profit, if the law allows them to do so.

The Gong of History; Or, What Is a Human?
Peter Linebaugh

EVERY GREAT HISTORICAL EPOCH in the freedom struggle raises the question: what is a human? The answer changes, to quote Askia Muhammad Toure of the Revolutionary Action Movement, with "the Gong of History." Amid all the confusing din of history, a note may sound that makes it audible and intelligible.

Yet the answer is always contested, and it may be lost in ideological noise. For instance, five hundred years ago, with the slaughter of millions of Native Americans, with the witch-burnings and demonization of women, with the voyages to Africa and the commencement of the Atlantic slave trade, the ideology of humanism functioned to cover up these crimes. French surrealists of the early twentieth century denounced Western humanism as justification of slavery, colonialism, and genocide in an essay called "Murderous Humanitarianism." Walter Johnson's critique of "the rights-based notion of the human being at the heart of the historiography of slavery" is part of this tradition. His broader project is to criticize the humanitarian excuses of neoliberal imperialism.

I want to make two general but related points. The first concerns "human" and the gong of history. The second concerns "capital" when history clangs.

JOHNSON QUOTES MARX'S ESSAY "On the Jewish Question," written in 1843, to show the limitations of "political emancipation"—*political* as opposed to *human*. I agree with this opposition, and I am sympathetic to Johnson's use of it to expose certain forms of humanism as imperial apologia, scholarly protocol, or neoliberal trope. But I do not think we should let these distortions have exclusive dibs on the human. A redemptive humanism is already implicit on the other side of the distinction Johnson invokes, and it is made fully explicit in Marx's writing of the following year. There we find a humanism that reaches back before the American Bill of Rights and the French Declaration of the Rights of Man and the Citizen, that sustained freedom struggles after the carnage of World War II, and that can guide us forward.

The Economic and Philosophic Manuscripts of 1844 were first translated into English in 1947 by Grace Lee Boggs, the Hegelian scholar in the workers' movement and close associate of C. L. R. James and Raya Dunayevskaya. The background to this important translation was war. Europe had shown itself capable of genocide within its own boundaries as well as in the colonial world. The oppressed people of Asia and Africa demanded liberation from European empires.

The humanism that emerged from these newly available Marx texts was the key to a trenchant postwar critique of the racism-capitalism nexus. Indeed "humanism" rather than "revisionism" was the watchword for those departing the orbit of the communist parties but who did not abandon revolutionary Marxism. At the heart of this humanism were

Marx's notions of labor and alienation, conceived as punishment and as suffering. "Production does not produce man only as a *commodity*, the *human commodity*, man in the form of a *commodity*," Marx wrote. "It also produces him as a *mentally* and physically *dehumanized* being." The crux was alienation: alienation from self, alienation from production, alienation from product, alienation from others. For Marx the opposite to this is "species-being," fully emancipated humanity. As Grace Lee Boggs's group Facing Reality would later write:

> Marx was concerned with the activity of the workers. By value production, he meant production which expanded itself through degradation and dehumanization of the worker to a fragment of a man. The essence of capitalist production is that it is a dynamically developing relation by which the dead labor in the machine, created by the workers, oppresses and degrades to abstract labor the living worker which it employs.

The solution was "the construction of a new society from the bottom up."

Looking quickly at the last two centuries, we can present the evolution of this humanism in three statements. Each arose from a massive movement of popular forces compelling the ruling class to respond with political repression, economic innovation, or imperial expansion. Each propelled the organized and spontaneous actions of the oppressed and exploited, giving heart where despair, fatalism, and servility had prevailed. And each line expressed a real or imagined African American voice. These summations arose from the struggle, and the struggle was forced to be not just a material but also a spiritual one.

The gong of history sounds thrice.

Am I Not a Man and a Brother?

IN 1787 ONE OF JOSIAH WEDGWOOD's craftsmen designed a cameo seal for the Abolition Society in London. Etched around a slave kneeling on one knee, unclothed but chained, is the question, "Am I Not a Man and a Brother?" Supplication on one knee indicates passage to Christianity; poor people knelt in church, while the rich did not. The "family of man" is suggested, as well as a secular notion of brotherhood, as in *fraternité*. The slogan summed up a movement that had been launched earlier, and it provided the standard to rally revolutionary developments in Haiti and France. Adam Hochschild cites this image of the supplicating—not rebellious—slave as among the many innovations of political organization and mobilization of public opinion.

Protestants led the formation of these abolitionist organizations: Olaudah Equiano, Thomas Clarkson, Ottobah Cugoano, Granville Sharp. Soon they broadened their focus to include issues of the working class as well, led by Thomas Hardy and Thomas Spence. In 1795 Spence struck a farthing with the Wedgwood's image and slogan on it. He wanted to make English spelling easier, public health universal, swimming pools required in every parish, and land equalized among everybody. His coinage quoted Milton, "Man over Man he made not Lord." Here, in short, was a conception of humanity that was anti-racist at the birth of "scientific" racism.

The seal spells out a question; it does not declare or propose an answer. Its tone is not declarative like that of the Bill of Rights or the French Declaration of Rights of Man and the Citizen, both of which came later and quickly succumbed to hypocrisy. It does not conceal a hidden political agenda, whether monarchy, republic, or commonweal. The gong of history sounded brotherhood. Women sounded it next.

Linebaugh

And Ar'n't I a Woman?

THIS IS THE QUESTION attributed in 1851 in Akron, Ohio, to the tall, gaunt black woman, Sojourner Truth, when she marched deliberately into the church where the Women's Convention was meeting, walking with "the air of a queen up the aisle [to] take her seat upon the pulpit steps." She whispered and thundered by turns.

"And how came Jesus into the world?" she asked in her speech to the group.

> Through God who created him and the woman who bore him. Man, where is your part? But the women are coming up blessed be God and a few of the men are coming up with them. But man is in a tight place, the poor slave is on him, woman is coming on him, and he is surely between a hawk and a buzzard.

Then, from her speech as remembered in 1863, she spoke of labor.

> I have plowed and planted and gathered into barns, and no man could head me—and ar'n't I a woman? I could work as much and eat as much as a man (when I could get it), and bear de lash as well—and ar'n't I a woman? . . . If de fust woman God ever made was strong enough to turn de world upside down all alone, dese women togedder (and she glanced her eye over the platform) ought to be able to turn it back, and get it right side up again!

To turn the world upside down was the revolutionary call by Paul against the Roman Empire, and it entered into the phraseology of the oppressed whenever hope joined desperation to produce historical miracles—the Peasants' Revolt, the English Revolution, National Liberations. In

Truth's formulation of the biblical stories, the mythic originator of sin—Eve—becomes the mythic savior of the world.

Her speech preceded the Civil War, the war of emancipation. It was during the war that the word "miscegenation" was coined to bad-mouth the Emancipation Proclamation of 1863 and to nullify the possibility of human beings of mixed race. This racist neologism was a political ploy against Lincoln and emancipation: it has done incalculable damage to the love of people of any color. The ugly term was a cunning semantic intervention against gender and sexual freedom.

No wonder that more than a hundred years later, black women might still suffer from "the feeling of craziness," as the Combahee River Collective Statement (1977) put it. The statement continued, "Above all else, our politics initially sprang from the shared belief that Black women are inherently valuable, that our liberation is a necessity not as an adjunct to somebody else's but because of our need as human persons for autonomy." The statement concluded, "This focusing upon our own oppression is embodied in the concept of identity politics. . . . We reject pedestals, queenhood, and walking ten paces behind. To be recognized as human, levelly human, is enough."

In that phrase, "levelly human," we hear faint reverberations from when the gong of history was struck by the Levellers, the radical abolitionists of the 1640s. It strikes again in 1968 in Memphis, Tennessee.

I Am a Man

BEFORE EMANCIPATION THE GONG of history asked questions; afterward it began to make declarations. "I Am a Man" was the slogan of the striking garbage and sewage workers of Memphis, led by AFSCME Local 1733 in April 1968. Commenting to the press, Reverend James Lawson said, "For at the heart of racism is the idea that a man is not a man, that a person is not a person. You are human beings. You are men. You deserve dignity." Lawson's words embody the message behind the strikers iconic placards, "I <u>Am</u> a Man." Dr. King joined the supporters the day before his assassination and spoke against starvation wages, reminding everyone that garbage and sewage workers benefited "humanity." The strikers were not claiming the rights of citizenship; their slogan was not "I Am a Citizen." Instead it expressed radical subjectivity.

IN THESE THREE SOUNDINGS of the gong of history we hear humanism, human nature, as historical rather than ontological. Its meaning is contested and in motion, an evolving construct of self-activity. These three variations of it—*fraternité*, sisterhood, and manhood—cannot be separated from the history that gave birth to them: the Haitian and French revolutions, the American Civil War, and the liberation movements of 1968 amidst the Vietnam War.

This brings me to my second general point, which concerns Johnson's notion of capital and his interpretation of Marx on this matter. He asks us to reconsider "the most basic distinction in political economy: the distinction between capital and labor." This is true of classical political economy, but it is not true of Marx's critique of political economy. Marx, like Johnson, says that the slaves were both capital and labor, drawing this conclusion from the fact that planters used slaves as collateral for loans.

Capitalism dehumanizes; one way it does so is by machines. This point is key to Marx but erased in Johnson's criticism of the rhetoric of dehumanization. Revolution by capital is the introduction of machines, "technological progress"; revolution *against* capital opposes this as oppressive and degrading. In 1957 Emmett Till was lynched and thrown in the Tallahatchie River with part of a cotton gin tied round his neck to sink him. In 1968 a mechanical malfunction crushed to death two sanitation workers, Echol Cole and Robert Walker, as they sought refuge from the rain in the back of their compressor trucks; Memphis city rules prohibiting refuge elsewhere. The Detroit auto proletariat fought this regime of the machine—of the reduction of men to machines, of the crushing of men by machines—by criticizing what they called "n----rmation." A forbidden term, the N-word, monkey-wrenched the classical discourse of political economy that separated labor and capital. As a political neologism of racist production, "n----rmation" resembles the political neologism of racialized reproduction, "miscegenation." Capital is not an inert thing of economic progress but a human relation of exploitation. To the worker, machines were deadly and could be torture. They clash with workers, even devour them. The gong of history discordantly clangs!

OTHER VARIATIONS OF HUMANISM as antidote to Marx's alienation arose throughout the later twentieth century. It played a significant role in the radical Zeitgeist expressed in French literature, Catholic philosophy, Protestant theology, and in the work of thinkers such as Erich Fromm, Herbert Marcuse, C. Wright Mills, and E. P. Thompson.

Fromm championed the "humanist socialism" of Georg Lukacs and Ernst Bloch. For him "the dehumanization of man" was evidenced by the cruelties of Hitler and Stalin. "The whole human race," he wrote in 1961, "is today the prisoner of the nuclear weapons it has created, and of the political institutions which are equally of its own making." The point is made very clearly by Mills:

> Marx is thoroughly and consistently humanist. A positive image of man, of what man might come to be, lies under every line of his analysis of what he held to be an inhuman society. His conception of 'alienation' alone—his analysis of the meaning of work under capitalism—is enough to reveal his humanism.

Thompson adapted the concept to the founding of the New Left in England in 1957. He left the Communist Party with a blazing attack on Stalinist ideology, and he did so in the name of "socialist humanism"—contrasting the "twisted inhumanity" of frozen ideological caricatures to "real men and women." He asserted "the humanist content of 'real' Communism," chronicling "the revolt against inhumanity, the revolt against dogmatism and abstraction of the heart."

It is true that, despite the chronological overlap between the American civil rights movement and the founding of the New Left, Thompson did not turn his attention to the alienation inherent in racism or to the humanity inherent in Black Power. Yet the socialist humanism of the New Left had profound influences. The Bandung conference of twenty-nine countries met in April 1955 to oppose colonialism and found the Non-Aligned Movement. Its ten-point program respected "fundamental human rights" and recognized "the equality of all races." The American activist and autoworker James Boggs spoke in 1970 of "the contradiction between the humane pretensions of this society, and its actual antihuman practices." To oppose American economic overdevelopment and political underdevelopment he called for "a new breed of socially and politically conscious and responsible human beings." Ella Baker likewise called for the rethinking and redefinition of most personal and intimate identities. For her, Barbara Ransby writes, "personal relations were key building blocks for a new, more human social order and for a successful revolutionary movement. It is in this sense that Ella Baker was a humanist." To create a new world, Baker says, "requires understanding that human beings are human beings."

The Revolutionary Action Movement was formed in Cleveland in 1962. It linked the struggle against racism in the United States with national liberation movements abroad. In 1965 it published an essay expounding the theory of "Bandung humanism" that placed the struggle between the Third World and imperialism as the central contradiction of the age, not the struggle between capital and labor. "How long," Toure asked, "does the white 'Free World' have before the Gong of History announces the Storm?"

Theories of Justice
Roberto Gargarella

RETHINKING OUR NOTION OF JUSTICE through the history of slavery is an appealing project, not least because it foregrounds what theories too easily forget: the agonies and abuses the most disadvantaged among us suffer. But it should also raise some concerns: about history, about human rights, and about justice.

History. The history of slavery does not narrate itself. We can all be shocked by the same images of violence, and we can all react with comparable levels of indignation in the face of racial exploitation. But the interpretive and theoretical nature of Johnson's project will require the use of other intellectual means and tools that make it subject to close scrutiny and critique.

Johnson rejects what he characterizes as a dominant approach to the history of slavery—one that, in casting twentieth-century liberalism as a foil, makes freedom the goal of justice. But both the dominant approach and Johnson's preferred one are idiosyncratic readings of slavery, conditioned by a whole array of pressures external to the subject matter itself. The profound contrast between the two approaches reveals the need to carefully examine and understand the history, not just the historiography. It also suggests the difficulties that belong to this enterprise and the reasonable divergences that may emerge.

It would be wrong, in any case, to choose between the dominant approach and alternatives by asking what is gained by thinking one way or the other, or by deciding which approach is less harmful, or by considering which produces the best consequences for some other purpose or inquiry. We should solve our factual and historical disagreements by thinking about which approach offers the best reconstruction of what actually happened.

Finally, even if we accept Johnson's contestable assumption that the dominant approach to the history of slavery presents a "dehumanized" view, his conclusions do not necessarily follow. For Johnson, the dominant approach presents "humanity as an aspect of the problem of freedom," and freedom as "the freedom to make choices and take intended actions—in other words, the bourgeois freedoms of classic liberalism." This account looks shoehorned. Is this really a fair assessment of dominant accounts of abolitionism and its legacy, including the civil rights movement? Where, for example, is Martin Luther King, Jr.? Couldn't we say that the dehumanization narrative (if that is even a correct characterization) makes a call for equality? Couldn't we say that these studies remind us, in the end, of the importance of recognizing that no part of humanity should be treated as possessing less moral worth? Why should we conclude that the dominant approach only makes a call for freedom, much less freedom in such restrictive terms?

Human Rights. Following Marx, Johnson rejects the idea that human rights represent the "final form of human emancipation." For him it is a species of "liberal neo-imperialism, the justifying terms of continuing

European and American intervention in the affairs of former colonies." For sure, the rhetoric of human rights has been repeatedly misused and abused by authoritarian leaders and in the service of political power. However, as a law professor from Latin America, I find Johnson's approach highly biased at best. The fact that governments in Latin America almost unanimously endorsed human rights discourse in the wake of dictatorships that devastated Latin America during the 1970s represents a fundamental collective achievement in advancing the rights of the most disadvantaged. Since the early 1980s, in fact, a majority of countries in the region incorporated different human rights treaties into their internal law. In some countries, such as Argentina and Bolivia, such treaties were explicitly awarded the status of constitutional laws. In other cases, such as Costa Rica or El Salvador, the treaties gained supra-legal status. As a consequence of the legal changes that followed, among other reasons, human rights began to gain life in real efforts to create more just societies.

Some initial examples: since the restoration of democracy, and in an unprecedented decision, Argentina began to prosecute hundreds of military officers who had taken part in the "dirty war" during the 1970s. General Pinochet was finally condemned and repudiated in Chile. In Brazil a national truth commission denounced the illegal arrests, torture, execution, and forced disappearances once performed by state agents. In Uruguay, once and again, massive social demonstrations have demanded respect for human rights.

Some other examples: the International Labor Organization's Convention 169 gave aboriginal groups the right to "prior consultation," with the objective of achieving agreement or consent to land use—such as logging, agribusiness, or mining projects—in indigenous territories. As a consequence, the Colombian Constitutional Court invalidated the national government's mining policy for violating the rights of

Afro-Colombian groups, and the Inter-American Court condemned Ecuador's mining policies for violating both the right to consultation and the physical integrity of members of the indigenous community of Sarayaku.

Such actions and decisions in the last few decades constitute just a few illustrations of the role played by human rights law. This is hard to square with Johnson's suggestion that human rights reflect just another form of "liberal neo-imperialism." Of course the path to the full realization of human rights is long and difficult. But in Latin America we conceive of human rights as allies, rather than obstacles or distractions in the fight for human justice; we see them as part of the solution, not part of the problem.

Justice. In the final part of his essay, Johnson enumerates six advantages of his alternative account of justice. But these features do not directly or naturally derive from the study of the history of slavery. They refer to preexistent values, related to a particular theory of justice—a theory of justice that undoubtedly many people, including myself, find attractive, but an independent theory nonetheless. As a result, those values, goals, and ideas of justice should be defined and defended independent of any account of the history of slavery. If we think it proper or better to criticize history from the standpoint of the "Global South," we should give reasons for that; if we want our notion of justice to be "attentive to questions of gender and sexuality," we should explain why. And if we want to defend a notion of justice attentive to questions of gender, we should do so regardless of whether the history of slavery calls attention to the issue. Even if our reading of that history did not inform the problems we care about, we would still have reasons for defending a theory of justice that is attentive, say, to questions of sexuality. We certainly should not go to the history looking to find in it a theory we are at pains to defend.

Johnson's view of justice seems largely Marxist in spirit, which some of us may find appealing. But this leads him to emphasize certain values to the exclusion or discounting of others. For instance, his reading of history does not pay much attention to social relationships, community values and practices, hierarchy and traditions, rituals, social bonds, religion, spirituality, and many other aspects of the lives of slaves that many would find indispensable to understanding their ideals and ways of life. The fact that Johnson focuses on gender and sexuality rather than traditional values, hierarchy, or communal practices says more about his preferred theory of justice, which should be presented and defended in full, than it says about the history of slaves under capitalism.

Racial Capitalism and the Dark Proletariat
Peter James Hudson

OUR IDEA OF RACIAL CAPITALISM, as Walter Johnson explains, comes from Cedric Robinson's *Black Marxism* (1983). But it has another lineage, one that predates Robinson even as it emerges from the same tradition of black radical thought to which he belonged.

In October 1979 an unsigned essay titled "Neo-Marxism and the Bogus Theory of 'Racial Capitalism'" appeared in *Ikwezi: A Black Liberation Journal of South African and Southern African Political Analysis*. Published in London, the journal offered a radical alternative to the politics of both the African National Congress and the South African Communist Party. *Ikwezi*'s take on racial capitalism is clear from the title: the concept is not to be celebrated and embraced as a critical counterweight to European Marxism. Instead it is a product of European Marxists' attempts to co-opt and condition black liberation struggles in southern Africa.

The essay argues, in particular, that the theory is a flawed "revisionist" strain of the South African Communist Party's clunky attempts to build on the models of "internal colonialism" and "colonialism of a special type" that were deployed to understand the South African situation. The journal saw racial capitalism as "counter-revolutionary clap-trap" espoused by "opportunistic" white leftists seeking to play a leading role in the Azanian liberation struggles. *Ikwezi* located the origins of the concept in the "revisionist" thought of "dubious, white" South African Marxists, in European "Neo-Marxists" and "euro-communist" philosophers such as Nicos Poulantzas and Ernest Mandel, in the "Trotskyite" analyses of the *New Left Review*, and in the pages of the *Review of African Political Economy*—especially its 1979 special issue on "The South African Situation," edited by Ruth First and Gavin Williams.

The essay saves most of its ire for the pamphlet *Foreign Investment and the Reproduction of Racial Capitalism in South Africa*, written by white South African Marxists Martin Legassick and David Hemson and published by the London-based Anti-Apartheid Movement in 1976. Legassick and Hemson misread the historical development of capitalism in South Africa, the *Ikwezi* essay argues, while downplaying the history of British and Dutch colonialism. The two men also marginalize the black worker as the subject of South African history by replacing him with a universal working-class subject with equal claim to the spoils of and struggle against apartheid and global capitalism. The proper analysis of the South African situation, *Ikwezi* says, can be found in the work of Lenin and "Comrade J.V. Stalin," and any theory that claims South Africa's racial orders emerge out of capitalist organization is mistaken. "To anyone familiar with the correct analysis of the Azanian liberation struggle," *Ikwezi* asserts, "the contention that racialism is a creation of capitalism and can only be overthrown by a proletarian revolution is a load of shit."

Ikwezi gets it wrong in many ways. Legassick and Hemson do not argue that South African "racialism" was the "creation of capitalism." They argue instead that modern manifestations of racism were historically contingent on the shifting regimes of capital accumulation in South Africa and the response of the South African state to it. They suggest that the racism of British colonialism and Dutch settler colonialism was reorganized with the nineteenth-century discovery of gold in the Witwatersrand, with South Africa's early twentieth-century industrialization, and with its attempts to secure multinational investment capital after the formal adoption of apartheid in 1949. Legassick and Hemson use the concept of racial capitalism to critique South African liberals who argued that apartheid was a "dysfunctional" aberration of capitalism that could be abolished through the improvement and better organization of South African capitalism—a position shared by many white South African capitalists, by Henry Kissinger and the U.S. State Department, and by the World Bank and the International Monetary Fund.

Despite *Ikwezi*'s protests, the theory of racial capitalism found a home within the writing of many South African activists and intellectuals who had emerged with the Pan Africanist Congress and within the Black Consciousness movement, especially in the wake of the Soweto Uprising. The most prominent figure in this regard was Neville Alexander, an activist and academic from the Eastern Cape involved in the Azanian People's Organization, the Cape Action League, and the National Forum Committee. Alexander's *One Azania, One Nation: The National Question in South Africa* (1979) grappled with the languages of race and nation used by the South African opposition, despairing at the reliance on the categories of the ruling national party and seeking a new political vocabulary. He is critical of the theoretical limits of both Marxism and Black Consciousness—the economic focus of one, the idealism of the other—and he laments the retrogressive and anachronistic statements of *Ikwezi*, viewing them as mired in contradiction and chauvinism. Alexander does not use the term "racial capitalism" in *One Azania* but, according to Nigel Gibson, he introduced it into the rhetoric of Black Consciousness. In his speech at the National Forum Committee convention in Hammanskraal in 1983, racial capitalism takes center stage. "The struggle against apartheid is no more than a point of departure for our liberatory efforts," he said. "Apartheid will be eradicated with the system of racial capitalism."

The force of Alexander's critique is directed, in part, to those who argued for the development of "non-racialism" or "multiracialism" in South Africa without first criticizing the underlying notions of immutable races—and without, at the same time, understanding the political-economic relations that shaped them. Non-racialism differed little from multiracialism; both relied on National Party definitions of race, and neither contained a critique of imperialism or capitalism. "A non-racial capitalism is impossible in South Africa," Alexander wrote. The future of South Africa was in an anti-racist socialism that could dismantle racial capitalism.

There are differences between the racial capitalisms of Robinson and of Alexander, Leggassick, and Hemson. While the South Africans particularize, Robinson universalizes. For Alexander, racial capitalism allows for the apprehension of the unique, indeed, the exceptional character of South Africa. It shows how the political economy of white supremacy in South Africa differed from that of the rest of the continent, and, for that matter, of the United States. For Robinson, though, racial capitalism is a global phenomenon. It is not limited to a particular nation-state, and it emerges at the beginning of European expansion. There are also methodological differences between Robinson's use of racial capitalism and its appearance in the South African context. This is most striking in the work of Leggassick and Hemson. While *Black Marxism* is a work of political philosophy, *Foreign Investment* is a work of political economy—perhaps the most sophisticated example we have of a text attempting to use racial capitalism as political-economic method.

It is tempting to imagine a set of possible exchanges, influences, and inferences through which Alexander and Robinson were sharing notes and ideas. Certainly Robinson was well aware of the global anti-apartheid struggle. In a 1980 review in *Contemporary Sociology*, he penned a withering critique of the collection *Race and Politics in South Africa* (there, he uses the term "apartheid capitalism"). And his essay "An Inventory of Contemporary Black Politics," published in *Emergency* in the early 1980s, contained a brief section on the history of multiracial organizing in the South African liberation struggle. Furthermore, his time in England at the end of the 1970s placed him at the center of a current of the global anti-apartheid struggles and of debates concerning black anti-racist and anti-imperialist politics in England. The London-based radical publisher Zed Books printed both Alexander's *One Azania, One Nation* and Robinson's *Black Marxism* while the journal *Race & Class*, published by the Institute of Race Relations, regularly featured Robinson's work along with pieces on the situation in southern Africa.

More important than intellectual genealogy is the simultaneous emergence of the theory in different places out of parallel—indeed, overlapping—conditions. In this homology we have a sense of the functioning of the black radical tradition—what Johnson describes as "the democratic practices and revolutionary thought of black people living under conditions of racial capitalism"—not as mystical power but as a historical-material force. This simultaneity links the modern experience of black people globally, yoked together across space and compressed into the same time through the machinery of global capitalism, global white supremacy. Tellingly, despite the South African exceptionalism of Alexander's work, he drew not only on the nation-building experiences in Guinea-Bissau and Mozambique for intellectual inspiration, but also on the theories of race developed by Gunnar Myrdal and the black sociologist Oliver Cromwell Cox to understand the U.S. experience.

The theory of racial capitalism also forces us to foreground what Du Bois, in *Black Reconstruction in America* (1935), called the "dark proletariat": racialized toilers whose historical presence dislodges the pretension of a universal working-class subject, who is invariably white. Instead the struggle for freedom and justice begins with the black worker. "The emancipation of man is the emancipation of labor," wrote Du Bois, "and the emancipation of labor is the freeing of that basic majority of workers who are yellow, brown and black." In similar fashion, here is Alexander, anticipating Johnson's uses of Marx on emancipation:

> We have seen that the national bourgeoisie have failed to complete the democratic revolution. The middle classes cannot be consistent since their interests are, generally speaking and in their own consciousness, tied to the capitalist system. Hence only the black working class can take the task of completing the democratization of the country on its shoulders. It alone can unite all the oppressed and exploited classes.

At the same time, as black feminists have been telling us for years, if the universal subject of working-class history is a white man, that of black working-class history is always a black man. Johnson counteracts this error by centering black women in the history of the regimes of accumulation and reproduction that created the modern world. "The entire 'pyramid' of the Atlantic economy of the nineteenth century," he writes, "was founded upon the capacity of enslaved women's bodies: upon their ability to reproduce capital." Du Bois is more succinct: "The crushing weight of slavery fell on Black Women." Historians including Jennifer S. Morgan, Stephanie Smallwood, Thavolia Glymph, Deborah Gray White, Sarah Haley, and many, many others have written extensively on this history in the United States. In the South African context, Pumla Dineo Gqola, Zine Magubane, Nthabiseng Motsemme, Christine

Qunta, Dabi Nkululeko, and Tshepo Masango Chéry are carrying out parallel work. We are living through a moment, in the United States, in South Africa, and elsewhere in the black world, when the analysis of black feminism is needed more than ever. Yet we still revert to an unreconstructed vision of racial capitalism with the male worker as its subject—and black and white men as its scribes.

Reviving the Black Radical Tradition
Manisha Sinha

WALTER JOHNSON IS UPSET at the state of the historiography of slavery and rightly challenges uncritical talk of "dehumanization." In its most extreme iteration, a few have even likened enslavement to the domestication of animals. This logic would carry us all the way back to Aristotle, who described slaves as talking tools. Pro-slavery ideologues were fond of this idea, even though southern slaveholders exploited the "human capacities" of enslaved people—to labor, reproduce, and, in Johnson's more Genovesean formulation, "to bear witness, to provide satisfaction, to provide a living, human register of slaveholders' power."

To advance this critique, Johnson appropriates Cedric Robinson's thesis of racial capitalism. But he does not fully engage the antithesis of that social arrangement: what Robinson called the black radical tradition and W. E. B. Du Bois "the role black folk played" in reconstructing democracy. Radical black scholars and activists—from Robinson, Du Bois, and C. L. R. James to Claudia Jones, Ida B. Wells, Sterling Stuckey, and Vincent Harding—wrote histories not just of black oppression but also of resistance, a term that many historians of slavery and the African

American experience now consider passé. Indeed, Johnson does not use the word at all. It might have an old-fashioned Marxist ring to it, but it has proven fruitful and capacious in the hands of such contemporary scholars of black politics and art as Eric Foner, Nell Painter, Steven Hahn, and Robin D. G. Kelley. These writers are heirs to a tradition that stretches back, in my reckoning, to African American abolitionists: Phillis Wheatley, Sojourner Truth, David Walker, Henry Highland Garnet, Frederick Douglass, Frances Harper, and Martin Delany. The richness of this lineage is missing from Johnson's account even though, following Kelley, he acknowledges its contemporary activist formulation in the Movement for Black Lives' broad-ranging manifesto, "A Vision for Black Lives."

Writing in these pages last year, Peter Hudson took to task several recent books on slavery and capitalism for neglecting the black radical tradition. The problem with such "deracialized historiography," Hudson argues, is that it views slaves mainly as objects of slaveholders' power or as quintessential victims of the rise of capitalism, foreclosing "the recovery of black resistance." Johnson clearly wrestles with this issue—whether or how to "recover" resistance—in the second half of his essay. On the one hand, the dehumanization argument carries with it the condescending notion that it is the historian's task to assign "agency" and grant "humanity" to enslaved people, as if that were possible. Johnson argues that these attempts are symptomatic of "simple-minded notions of moral progress" that replace "histories of perpetration" with bourgeois notions of freedom and human rights, a discourse that he ascribes, with Samuel Moyn, to a neo-imperialist liberalism of the middle and late twentieth century. On the other hand, Johnson himself claims to speak from an "ethical dimension" in calling for a renewal of bottom-up history and a more robust Marxist notion of human emancipation.

This brings us back to Marx, and rightly so. But any appreciation of Marxism must begin with the recognition that, despite the attempts of scores of conservative writers and thinkers to write Marx out of the development of Western humanism, he was in fact a product—the logical endpoint, some might say—of Enlightenment thought. For Marx, capitalism was a revolutionary force that destroyed centuries of tradition—archaic economic structures such as feudalism and slavery—in a teleological historical schema. Even the tyranny of European imperialism, he argued, destroyed still more tyrannical systems, which he termed "Asiatic despotism." Marx understood the human cost of slavery, capitalism, and imperialism better than any other Western radical thinker of his time, but he wrote from the vantage point of a nineteenth-century European. It has taken generations of other thinkers and revolutionaries—including V. I. Lenin, Rosa Luxemburg, and M. N. Roy—to extend Marx's insights about the history of imperialism, just as it has taken generations of black scholars and activists—including Robinson, Du Bois, and James—to do the same for the history of slavery and race.

Capitalism, in this deepened understanding, was hardly a force of progressive destruction, ushering in the dawn of communism. It not only reinforced old structures of oppression but also created its own barbaric forms of exploitation. Nor has it always promoted the growth of democracy; in most cases it has led to the evisceration of democratic norms and principles. (Marx himself made this point in his brilliant *The Eighteenth Brumaire of Louis Napoleon*, a history of the fall of the French Second Republic.) The bourgeoisie is neither democratic nor progressive, contrary its depictions in the long-enthroned, antiseptic, and whitewashed narratives of Anglo-American history. Like all ruling classes in history, it tends to be reactionary and anti-democratic, happy to consort with aristocrats, slaveholders, and fascists when the opportunity arises. It is stingy when it comes to democracy, citizenship, and rights, drawing rigid lines of nationality, race, class, and gender. In short, the advance of democracy in the world, Western or otherwise, has very little to do with elites and a lot to do with the demands of the subaltern, however we may define them.

To dismiss the idea of universal human rights as bourgeois folly is thus an academic exercise, a lily-white conceit unmindful of the history of the black liberation struggles and anti-imperialist movements that were much more important to its emergence in the mainstream than some self-actualizing trajectory of liberalism in the West. The lion's share of the credit belongs not to liberals but to the black radical tradition and the critique of Western imperialism emerging from the Global South, Africa, Asia, and Latin America. This is the reason black radicals—such as Du Bois and others who took part in the Pan-African Congress—saw anti-racism in the United States and anti-imperialism as two sides of the same coin. And, yes, these movements do connect to the Western tradition epitomized by Thomas Paine, Marx, and interracial abolitionism. Long before the United Nation's Universal Declaration of Human Rights (1948), abolitionists had made human rights a touchstone for resisting the racialist laws of the slaveholding republic. That is why black activists from Du Bois and Paul Robeson to Malcolm X and Black Lives Matter have sought to bring their country to the bar of international public opinion and the UN on charges of violating human rights.

The erasure of this history is both pervasive and insidious. Some radical scholars in the West have perhaps been just as guilty of Eurocentrism as their liberal counterparts in dismissing "third world nationalism" and movements against racial injustice as essentialist, alien and foreign to some pristine nationalist left traditions of their own. In the United States this thinking masquerades as a critique of "identity politics," unmindful of the interconnectedness—or to use a more fashionable term, intersectionality—of racial, gendered, and economic injustice and struggles. The truth is that unless we develop a politics of resistance that marries the internationalism of early Marxism with the very particular history of racial liberation struggles all over the world—something that black radical activists and "third world" revolutionaries have actually attempted to do—we are doomed.

It is high time, then—as we theorize and return to the insights of racial capitalism—that we situate our discussion of emancipation in the very specific black radical tradition that Robinson and Du Bois evoked. When we write new histories of slavery and capitalism, we need to revive both the history and the ongoing political project of black liberation. If histories of capitalism have been willfully blind to slavery, race, and imperialism, they are "equally blind to the emancipatory possibilities of the black radical tradition which emerged in opposition to it," as Paul Hebert put it in a recent forum on Robinson's *Black Marxism* on the African American Intellectual History Society's blog. This tradition has a lot to tell us about the theory and praxis of resistance. (That does not mean it should be immune to critique. In the same forum, Carol Boyce Davies notes the erasure of African American women, and issues of gender and sexuality more generally, from a masculinist construction of resistance.)

In writing these new histories, we must be sensitive to our own historical exigencies. As Robinson noted, "The resoluteness of the black radical tradition advances as each generation assembles the data of its experience to an ideology of liberation." There is a telling illustration of this advancement in the disagreement between C. L. R. James and Eric Williams. Though he sharply analyzed the central role of slavery in the emergence of capitalism, Williams viewed abolition as a bourgeois, metropolitan business decision to shift resources from an allegedly bankrupt slave system to industrial capitalism. James, by contrast, restored the Haitian Revolution to the history of global abolition in his seminal work *The Black Jacobins*, and Du Bois made the slaves' general strike central to the story of Civil War emancipation—two important steps in recovering the significance of the black radical tradition in the history of abolition and emancipation. It is notable, as Matthew Quest has detailed in *Insurgent Notes*, that James criticized Williams's book for leaving out "the liberating activity of the slaves themselves." Only by writing people of African descent out of the history of abolition can we view it as a white, bourgeois movement designed to justify capitalism and, later, imperialism. Only by writing the non-white world out of the history of democracy and human rights can we develop narrow and ahistorical genealogies of their emergence and progress in the modern Western world, which since its conception has been interracial.

Robinson puts it best in *Black Marxism*: the enslaved "constituted one of the crucial social bases in contradiction to bourgeois society." Radical social movements, including abolitionism, "generate new knowledge, new theories, new questions," Robin Kelley further notes in *Freedom Dreams*: "The most radical ideas often grow out of a concrete intellectual engagement with the problems of aggrieved populations confronting systems of oppression." Johnson's concluding prescriptions have long historical antecedents, too easily forgotten and frequently misunderstood.

Putting Rights in Their Place
Samuel Moyn

WALTER JOHNSON GIVES A BRACING critique of two ways of telling the history of slavery. One uses the rhetoric of humanity, the other the contemporary discourse of human rights. Rejecting both these trends on ethical grounds, Johnson offers an alternative vision of politics—and thus an alternative way of writing history. By and large I agree with him, but sometimes for other reasons than he gives.

Take "humanity" first. Johnson insists that not only did victims of oppression never risk losing their humanity (an offensive question in the first place, underwritten by the logic of white supremacy); masters did not betray their own humanity, either. Instead, slavery illustrates precisely what humans so often and so willingly do to other humans. Our bleak history is not one of dehumanization or inhumanity, but instead of the all too human capacity for domination.

To this argument some will object that we must attend to the way oppressors view their own activity. After all, their goals have often been self-consciously to dehumanize. In his recent depictions of slavery across the ages, for example, historian David Brion Davis, following a classic essay by Karl Jacoby, explains that from Aristotle forward, slavery was often imagined to reduce people in bondage to the status and functions of (non-human) animals. And, as Terrence Des Pres and others have written, in Nazi camps Germans deliberately aimed at robbing Jews of their basic humanity.

But Johnson is right to worry about overinterpreting this fact. For one thing, studying the rhetoric used by oppressors does not require that we embrace it ourselves; indeed the very uses to which it has been put would seem to demand the skepticism of the historian. For another thing, engaging that very rhetoric traps liberals in a worrisome dialectic. Those who plangently retort that victims keep their humanity, Johnson bitterly records, look away not just from their bondage but also from all the forms of subordination that have proven compatible with formal emancipation. The issue is how narrowly liberals have conceived of the humanity they claim to recognize in victims. To Johnson, the liberal recognition of the agency and autonomy of the enslaved is little more than a "bourgeois" attempt to redeem victims from their past or present oppression—as if racial capitalism did not still oppress so many. And insisting on the inhumanity of the enslavers sets up domination as the unlikely exception rather than the enduring rule.

As I see it, Johnson offers this critique of a too narrow conception of humanity in order to provoke the formulation of a broader one, not to insist that we must dispense with talk of humanity altogether. Others have come to more severe conclusions. Contemporary Italian philosopher Giorgio Agamben, for example, argues that oppression (Auschwitz, in his reading) actually did succeed in turning humans into non-humans, and that it is for this very reason that we must relinquish the normative ideal of humanity once and for all. (What should replace it, in Agamben's analysis, is not so clear.) It seems to me that Johnson does not quite make this leap; he merely wishes to lay the groundwork for a humanism that takes seriously the enduring injustices of racial capitalism. His target is not humanism *tout court* but a particular, if powerful and entrenched, brand of humanism: the liberalism of those for whom the humanity of the formally enslaved matters, but not that of the informally and persistently oppressed. If bourgeois emancipation is faulty, Johnson says, it is because what Karl Marx called "human" emancipation might fulfill or better fulfill our interests. Johnson's critique of rights thus strikes me as more compelling than his critique of the rhetoric of humanity. His own premises suggest that we may need to keep the possibility of appealing to humanity around.

The other target of Johnson's critique is the new trend in scholarship to recast anti-slavery as a human rights movement *avant la lettre*. It is true that there was an uptick in the usage of the phrase "human rights" in English in the 1830s—though it was nothing to the salience it achieved in the late twentieth century—and that the French revolutionary slogan of the rights of man shaped discussions of slavery. As Evelyn Brooks Higginbotham has reminded us, William Lloyd Garrison's newspaper *The Liberator* had *Human Rights* as one of its alternate titles, and historians of various stripes—including Robin Blackburn, Jenny Martinez, Kathryn Kish Sklar, and Amy Dru Stanley—have made similar claims, either that the rhetoric of abolitionism featured appeals to individual rights or that the cause took the form of what we would now call a human rights movement.

But, like Johnson, I am skeptical. There is more reason—both historical and political—to minimize the resemblance between anti-slavery and contemporary human rights movements than to play it up.

To start, rights were the arsenal of the slaveholding class—primarily the sacrosanct right to property, as historian James Oakes has stressed when it comes to the American scene. Not that rights talk couldn't figure on the other side of the argument, but it was rarely central—perhaps because abolitionists knew that the appeal to rights, in itself, didn't settle any arguments in their favor. Even the invocation of rights on behalf of the enslaved was overwhelmingly restricted to national debates about whether blacks should count as fellow citizens. No one was trying to elevate rights to international law or to establish protections that would intrude upon national sovereignty—the hallmark of contemporary human rights as both an idea and an enterprise. When slavery was engaged beyond borders—for example, by a moralizing British public and state—it was rarely in terms of the human rights of slaves and frequently in frameworks that joined humanitarian pity and imperialist assumptions.

It is true that some of the techniques of abolitionism, either within nations or beyond borders, resemble those of contemporary human rights activism—from naming and shaming to consumer boycotts. The trouble with the comparison is that it selects for emphasis the forms and figures of anti-slavery that best approximate our own most familiar style of (nonviolent) agitation. Garrison, for example, is routinely credited as a human rights activist before his time, but John Brown never gets that designation. Worst of all, when we convert anti-slavery mobilization into human rights advocacy, slaves themselves—especially when they engaged in violent self-emancipation—simply drop out of the picture. Gone, apparently, are the days when, remembering the Haitian uprising in *The Black Jacobins*, C. L. R. James could dismiss human rights as some of the "wordy" promises of "eloquent phrasemakers" who, volunteering to "perorate" to mask their rule, were in the end willing to give up the aristocracy of the skin only when insurgents threatened violence.

It is now commonly believed that human rights are the natural responses to oppression. But the truth is that there are no such natural responses, whether ethical or practical; there are only contingent ones. How we interpret oppression when we recognize it at all is subject to a specific framework, and even if it is possible to name some frameworks as better and some worse, all are subject to critique and improvement. It is likewise almost universally assumed that the Holocaust prompted the annunciation of human rights in the Universal Declaration of Human Rights (1948) and European Convention on Human Rights (1950). That human rights seem so self-evident a response to horror says more about us than even our recent ancestors. As Marco Duranti has shown, hardly any of the advocates of the international annunciation of rights in the 1940s were specifically concerned with what the Jews had recently suffered. And at the time most Jews prioritized nationalism, in their old homes or new Jewish state; those who opted for some sort of internationalist retort to the horrors of German nationalism turned to socialism. The visibility of international human rights instead arose primarily in response to decolonization, out of the fear—sometimes justified—that fervent attacks on a white world order were perversely serving as pretexts for black despotism, with "nationalism" and "socialism" functioning as masks for the oppression of individuals. Deprived of imperialism, many liberals from the Global North rallied to the rhetoric of human rights to channel concern and spread opprobrium about suffering in the Global South.

While Johnson is right to resist the reduction of the attack on slavery and racial domination to the contemporary human rights movement, I think it is wrong to foreclose some future version of human rights that might escape its current limitations. Johnson himself says "it would be better" if human rights politics were "significantly inflected by the history of slavery," but when he comes to his own sketch of "an account of justice," there is no mention of what role such rights might have in it. Presumably the reason for this neglect is that individuals still suffer domination as part of collective groups, beyond the reach of rights-based remedies—a view Johnson rightly associates with the black Marxist tradition and its theory of racial capitalism, even if it is compatible with other approaches, too. What liberation from oppression modern history has witnessed so far has normally occurred through the collective self-assertion of peoples and classes, and at its most promising it reached out to all humanity as its agent and beneficiary. I infer from Johnson that what our current theories and practices of individual rights leave out are the ineluctably collective structures of oppression and the necessarily collective resistance that might break them. Individuals and their rights do have a place, indeed an essential one, in our most progressive understandings of oppression and emancipation, but it is a much smaller place than they have had lately. Current events demand this new understanding of the past, and the evidence most certainly allows it.

What Slavery Tells Us about Marx
Stephanie Smallwood

FOLLOWING W. E. B. DU BOIS and Cedric Robinson, Walter Johnson suggests that "the history of (racial) capitalism began with the slave trade rather than the factory system." When Johnson presented an earlier version of his essay at the "Future of the African American Past" conference at the Smithsonian Institution, he asked, "Of what ethical or analytical use is the term 'capitalism' if it cannot describe the world-making commodification and transportation of twelve million Africans to the New World?" Putting the slave trade (as distinct from antebellum slavery) at the center of our historical work can help, in particular, to clarify the ways Marx failed to adequately account for the origins of capitalism, and also illuminates the interpretive consequences of that failure.

It is worth noting that Marx fully recognized the Atlantic slave trade for what it was: a system of commercial trafficking in humans. In his discussion of "The Genesis of the Industrial Capitalist" in *Capital*, Marx wrote:

> The discovery of gold and silver in America, the extirpation, enslavement and entombment in mines of the indigenous population of that continent, the beginnings of the conquest and plunder of India, and the conversion of Africa into a preserve for the commercial hunting of blackskins, are all things which characterize the dawn of the era of capitalist production. These idyllic proceedings are the chief moments of primitive accumulation.

But Marx's placement of the slave trade in capitalism's prehistory of "primitive accumulation," even while acknowledging its commercial nature, sits at odds with another key instance where he addressed the subject of slave-trading. In his discussion of "The Working Day" in *Capital*, Marx observes, "Capital asks no questions about the length of life of labour-power," and turns to Irish liberal political economist J. E. Cairnes's study, *The Slave Power* (1863), for assistance in illustrating the point. In Cairnes's book, he precedes the passage Marx quotes by explaining that his purpose is "to direct attention, not so much to the barbarous inhumanity of the slave-trade, whether foreign or domestic, as to what has not been so often noticed—the mode in which it operates in giving increased coherence and stability to the system of which it is a part." He then continues with the sentences reproduced by Marx:

> The rice-grounds of Georgia, or the swamps of the Mississippi, may be fatally injurious to the human constitution; but the waste of human life which the cultivation of these districts necessitates, is not so great that it cannot be repaired from the teeming preserves of Virginia and Kentucky. Considerations of economy, moreover, which, under a natural system, afford some security for humane treatment by identifying the master's interest with the slave's preservation, when once trading in slaves is practised, become reasons for racking to the uttermost the toil of the slave; for, when his place can at once be supplied from foreign preserves, the duration of

his life becomes a matter of less moment than its productiveness while it lasts. It is accordingly a maxim of slave management, in slave-importing countries, that the most effective economy is that which takes out of the human chattel in the shortest space of time the utmost amount of exertion it is capable of putting forth. It is in the tropical culture, where annual profits often equal the whole capital of plantations, that negro life is most recklessly sacrificed. It is the agriculture of the West Indies, which has been for centuries prolific of fabulous wealth, that has engulfed millions of the African race.

Marx concludes his analysis, "*Mutato nomine de te fabula narratur* (The name is changed, but the tale is told of you)! For slave trade, read labour-market, for Kentucky and Virginia, Ireland and the agricultural districts of England, Scotland and Wales, for Africa, Germany." With this maneuver, Marx presents slave-trading in the Americas as *analogous* to the capitalist labor market in industrializing Europe that "produces the pre-mature exhaustion and death of this labour-power itself." It stands out as a moment of analytical slippage that makes his tendency to hold New World slavery apart from capitalism all the more glaring—not just for its gross imprecision, but also for the inevitable interpretive blunders to which it leads.

Throughout most of Marx's work, slavery's chief function is heuristic: it is an ahistorical foil against which to set capitalism's unique and singular excesses and inhumanity. Elsewhere in his discussion of "The Working Day," Marx depicts slavery in the South as having "preserved a moderately patriarchal character" for most of its history, as "production was chiefly directed to the satisfaction of immediate local requirements." Southern slavery is thus understood as having only recently become oriented toward "a world market dominated by the capitalist mode of production" and "sale of [slave-grown] products for export." In other words, it was the capitalist regime centered on cotton, and not slavery itself, that produced "the over-working of the Negro, and sometimes the consumption of his life in seven years of labour." Even Marx's often-cited figuring of New World slavery as the pedestal that grounds the veiled slavery of European capitalism retains the anachronistic framing of American slavery as having a benign past that was lost to the corroding influence of capital. For Marx, the overriding theme in the relationship between slavery and capitalism is that it was the latter that corrupted the former.

We have long since dismissed Marx's misunderstanding of slavery, but we have not reckoned sufficiently with the consequences of his error. Marx's failure to subject slavery to historical analysis led him away from an obvious interpretive conclusion: that slave-trading was analogous to the capitalist labor market because it gave birth to the capitalist mode of production. Oliver Cox pointed to this interpretive misstep when he observed, in *Capitalism as a System* (1964), that Marx "begins his analysis of the nature of capitalism almost where he might have ended it; and as is commonly the case in classical economics, he relegates as subsidiary the very things which should have been the center of his study. . . . His 'primitive accumulation' is none other than fundamentally capitalist accumulation."

Asking what the slave trade says about Marx requires that we start where Marx did, with analysis of the commodity form. But we need to replace the bolt of linen Marx used as the iconic object of that analysis—not with the slave-cultivated cotton that was more central to nineteenth-century industrial manufacturing; or even the slave-grown sugar that fueled the colonial wealth Marx erroneously identified as part of capitalism's prehistory. To heed Johnson's call to "use the history of slavery as the source rather than the subject of knowledge," we will have to instead put the enslaved human herself at the center of our analysis of the commodity form.

Putting the slave trade at the center of our analysis of racial capitalism leads also to an alternative understanding of what Marx described as the "historical movement which changes the producers into wage-labourers." If, as Lisa Lowe has argued in *The Intimacy of Four Continents* (2015), the promises of nineteenth-century discourses of liberalism were a ruse, we might need to more skeptically interrogate the received narrative of the transition from slavery to freedom. The "movement" to which Marx refers may not have been toward "emancipation," as he assumes throughout *Capital*, but rather a further refinement of capitalism's commodification of the human—which is to say, a reworking of slavery.

When Liberalism Defended Slavery
Andrew Zimmerman

WALTER JOHNSON DEMONSTRATES HOW little liberal humanism, with its celebration of individual rights and agency, has to offer those wishing to understand the history of slavery or seeking justice for communities that have survived enslavement. I would extend Johnson's critique by pointing out that liberal humanism has long been a central component of the political ideology of slaveholders and their allies and abettors. Overlooking this relationship of liberal humanism and slavery—seeing liberalism merely as an insufficient approach to slavery—means offering an incomplete critique of both.

Strange though it may seem today, liberalism—the political doctrine that attributed rights to individuals that no government, no matter how democratic or just, could violate—offered one of the most important legal and ideological protections for slavery in the nineteenth century. Liberalism defined rights as private, and the ultimate such right was the right to hold private property. Racism was, of course, central to the definition of some human beings as property. But liberalism meant that no matter what a legislator or judge thought of people of African descent or the morality of holding slaves, the state could not interfere with private property rights. In its infamous 1857 *Dred Scott v. Sandford* decision, the Supreme Court not only denied citizenship and rights to people of African descent, but also affirmed that slavery enjoyed the same constitutional protections as every other form of property-holding. Despite the genuine moral revulsion of many liberals toward slavery, the individual right to private property stymied efforts to overthrow it. We might say the same of liberal responses to any number of catastrophes we face today, from mass poverty to global climate change.

Affirmations of the special dignity of humanity also served to justify slavery. No less an authority than Aristotle reminded his elite male readers that their very humanity depended on slaves performing the labor necessary for their bodily survival, leaving them free to devote themselves to uniquely human pursuits. (For Aristotle these were philosophy, politics, and gymnastics.) The racism characteristic of European modernity only further bolstered this argument. The alleged dehumanization of enslaved people, which Johnson so rightly dismisses as empirically inaccurate and theoretically muddled, was also the ground of the alleged humanization of slaveholders. Humanity, for Aristotle—as well as for U.S. slavery apologists such as George Fitzhugh—was not a natural property of the human species but a ruling-class aspiration for the few that required the forced labor of the many.

That liberal humanism provided the central ideological perspective of white, middle-class abolitionists reveals the extent of their complicity in, if not precisely racial slavery, then the hierarchy of people and property of which racial slavery was a component. There is perhaps no better illustration of this than the first issue of the great middle-class anti-slavery newspaper, William Lloyd Garrison's *Liberator*. There we find a brief denunciation of David Walker's *Appeal . . . to the Colored Citizens of the World* (1829), the famous pamphlet calling for armed resistance to the racist exploitation of African Americans in slave as well as wage labor. Immediately adjacent, a short editorial inveighs against those who would "inflame the minds of our working classes against the more opulent." It was not working-class enemies of slavery but middle-class abolitionists who separated race and class, slavery and capitalism—the better to immunize the latter from the critiques of the former. The concept of racial capitalism, by contrast, reminds us that there is no viable analysis of racism or of capitalism that treats either in isolation.

For this reason I wholly agree with Johnson that scholars and activists should follow Cedric Robinson's *Black Marxism*. I think doing so requires developing not just Robinson's concept of racial capitalism, but also his concept of a black radical tradition in a complex dialogue with Marxism.

As Johnson suggests, what Robinson analyzed as the black radical tradition offers a more promising perspective than liberal humanism for understanding slavery and combatting ongoing racial capitalism. For Robinson this tradition was not simply a response to racial capitalism or enslavement; it had African roots prior to, and independent of, the forms of oppression it combatted. "The Black radical tradition," he wrote, "casts doubt on the extent to which capitalism penetrated and re-formed social life and on its ability to create entirely new categories of human experience stripped bare of the historical consciousness embedded in culture. . . . After all it had been as an emergent African people and not as slaves that Black men and women had opposed enslavement." Robinson does not reduce the black radical tradition to a static, ahistorical, unitary culture; that is why he refers to an "*emergent* African people" comprised of many different cultures and classes and a broad range of cultural and political productions, from the social healing practices of Obeah, Vodou, and other Afro-Atlantic religions to the writings of contemporary black intellectuals.

It is in the black radical tradition that we can locate a humanism separate from—indeed antithetical to—the liberal, rights-bearing individualism that Johnson has so powerfully criticized. In his *Discourse on Colonialism* (1955), the Martiniquan intellectual Aimé Césaire marveled at the racism of those who both recoiled in horror at the atrocities the Nazis carried out in Europe and yet had long accepted similar atrocities in their own colonial empires. (In Africa those European colonial atrocities also found justification in a liberal humanist mission that claimed—falsely—to stamp out slavery while promoting "Christianity, Commerce, and Civilization.") Césaire thus called for "a true humanism —a humanism made to the measure of the world." This humanism would, for Césaire, result from communist revolutions, especially by black workers, who had been "doubly proletarianized and alienated."

In the thick of the Algerian revolution, Césaire's former pupil, Frantz Fanon, understood perhaps better than any how to practice the true humanism his teacher had called for: relentless anti-colonial and anti-capitalist revolution. For Fanon, humanism was accessible only via nationalism—one "explained, enriched, and deepened" (rather than abandoned, overcame, or transcended). Here Fanon's nationalism converges with Robinson's black radical tradition as well as with Marxism and the communist parties and states that supported decolonization. Césaire, Fanon, and so many other great luminaries of the tradition, including Robinson himself, were absolutely clear about the importance of communism and Marxism to their work against colonialism and racism.

Here I find myself disagreeing with Johnson, who, like Robinson, proposes what I regard as an overly sharp distinction between "orthodox" Marxism and the black radical tradition. To be sure, these are distinct traditions, but even what Johnson calls (verging on caricature) "uninflected Marxism" is far more capacious, far less "authoritarian," than he allows.

The Marxist position that Johnson describes as orthodox appears to be that of the U.S. historian Eugene Genovese, who, unlike Marx and most mainstream Marxists, held that American slavery was a pre-capitalist social formation. Genovese's position has its roots in a late nineteenth-century dispute between Marxists and Populists in Russia. Russian Marxists at that time insisted that Russian agriculture needed first to pass through a stage of capitalism before a transition to socialism could be contemplated, whereas Populists held that Russian peasants could build socialism directly, on the basis of their communal landholdings. Lenin, at least until the October Revolution, held on to the stage theory of his Marxist comrades. Marx himself, however, sided with the Populists in his 1881 letter to Vera Zasulich.

Throughout his long career, Marx emphasized that, while slavery had existed for most of human history, the enslavement of people of African descent in the Americas was a unique and integral component of modern global capitalism. He stated this clearly in *Poverty of Philosophy* (1847), and it remained a theme of constant, growing importance in his subsequent work, from his voluminous writings on the U.S. Civil War, through, as Kevin Anderson has recently shown, the three volumes of *Capital*. Though it has long been rejected by most Marxists, the stage theory that characterizes slavery as pre-capitalist continues to flourish among liberal modernization theorists in the World Bank, International Monetary Fund, and elsewhere.

Whatever the merits of Genovese's account of U.S. slavery as pre-capitalist, taking it as Marxist orthodoxy—whether in praise or condemnation—mischaracterizes Marxism. In doing so it sets Marxism at odds with the black radical tradition, which has long been one of its most important interlocutors. What Johnson says of James Oakes's counterfactual, "science fiction" account of capitalism without slavery could also be said of Johnson's account of a Marxism without Césaire and Fanon, as well as W. E. B. Du Bois, C. L. R. James, and so many others. We should take seriously that flash of the future that Du Bois glimpsed in the past, in the revolution of African American workers in the South during and after the Civil War: "one of the most extraordinary experiments of Marxism that the world, before the Russian revolution, had seen."

Scholars elsewhere in the Americas have been less likely than those in the United States to classify slavery as pre-capitalist, a relic from the past. In the 1960s Andre Gunder Frank analyzed what he called "the development of underdevelopment" to show that the economic forms that liberal modernizers characterized as backward or primitive are in fact coeval components of an international capitalist division of labor. More recently, scholars rooted in the related field of World Systems Theory, including Dale Tomich and Michael Zeuske, have analyzed how capitalism and slavery developed together, particularly in the industrial transformation of plantation production in nineteenth-century Cuba.

The Peruvian sociologist Anibal Quijano has built on the work of scholars in this tradition to offer a profound explanation of racial capitalism in the Americas. According to Quijano, European colonizers in the Americas were the first to bring together a variety of already existing forms of labor coercion, from serfdom and slavery to independent craft production and wage labor, around a racial division of labor and for the purposes of capital accumulation. Capitalism and racism, Quijano suggests, emerged simultaneously, and originally, in the Americas. Refinements of manufacturing techniques in the northwest corner of Europe, so often imagined as capitalism proper, are, by comparison, trivial.

For these reasons I share Johnson's sense of the importance of Marxism and the black radical tradition, not just for what they tell us about capitalism, but also for the role they play in the struggles for justice against racial capitalism's exploitation and oppression. I wonder, though, whether justice is yet another of those terms, along with agency and humanity, clustered around a liberalism too bound to racial capitalism to understand or overthrow it. As Ava DuVernay emphasized in her documentary *13th*, the system of justice we have in the United States has been tasked by the Thirteenth Amendment with transferring human bondage from the plantation to the prison. The amendment explicitly permits "slavery" and "involuntary servitude," after all, as "a punishment for crime whereof the party shall have been duly convicted."

Césaire denounced the racism of Eurocentric humanism to call for a "humanism made to the measure of the world," and we in the United States ought to denounce our own racist justice system to call for a justice made to the measure of the world. But we should also consider the mechanics and practicalities of bringing justice to justice, much as Césaire proposed bringing humanism to humanism. For thinkers such as Césaire and Marx, the transition from the merely formal to the truly human occurs not simply by completing the work of the (necessarily racist, imperialist, enslaving) bourgeoisie. It occurs through revolution.

Black Humanity and Black Power
Peniel Joseph

BLACK HUMANITY IS UNEXCEPTIONAL, Walter Johnson exhorts. Once we have taken up the debate of humanization versus dehumanization under slavery, we have already ceded critical ground. Like Johnson, midcentury Black Power activists understood that it was necessary to redirect such questions toward the matter of how the legacy of racial slavery continues to shape citizenship, democratic participation, and human rights, not just for black Americans but for people of color around the globe. Johnson's essay offers profitable avenues for reappraising how Black Power is the conceptual bridge between Reconstruction-era black struggles for self-determination and Black Lives Matter's present-day fight to end martial and economic violence against people of color.

One of the most critical contributions of the Black Power movement was its searing critique of American racial capitalism. The movement's roots in multiple strands—black nationalist, black feminist, black Marxist—of the black radical tradition formed the basis of its understanding of political revolution, community organizing, and the links between local, national, and global human rights struggles. Inspired in part by

Nation of Islam theology—which holds the foundational belief that people of color are the most fully human of all—Malcolm X, Black Power's political and ideological avatar, predicated his political ideology on the conviction that slavery's legacy is central in shaping contemporary racial oppression.

Stokely Carmichael, the charismatic Student Nonviolent Coordinating Committee (SNCC) chairman who emerged as the de facto leader of Black Power, spent years living and organizing among black sharecroppers in the Mississippi Delta and Alabama, from which he gained firsthand knowledge of how the legacies of slavery continued well into the twentieth century. Carmichael responded by preaching a vision of radical self-love, one that defiantly promoted black beauty, insisted on the value of African and African American history, and traced America's imperial mission back to racial slavery. Indeed, for Carmichael black sharecroppers in Mississippi—for example, the Mississippi Freedom Democratic Party organizer Fannie Lou Hamer—offered America its most humane face and best hope for unshackling itself from its shameful past. And like Malcolm, Carmichael presupposed black humanity, which contoured his political activism and intellectual worldview.

If the respectability politics infusing aspects of civil rights activism relied on African Americans performing humanity in a never-ending audition before a skeptical white audience, Black Power activists flipped this dynamic on its head. Recognizing racial capitalism as the purveyor of evils that transcended the U.S. nation-state, Carmichael traveled through the Caribbean, Africa, and Europe exposing long-buried but now self-evident links between American incursions in Vietnam, institutional racism at home, and global practice of white supremacy, which hold the uncanny ability to shape political, cultural, and economic systems while overdetermining the parameters of their opposition.

Likewise contemptuous of respectability politics and the endless auditioning of one's humanity, the Black Panthers sought to alter the entire landscape of black political engagement by delegitimizing the U.S. nation-state, which they characterized as bankrupt due to racial slavery, institutional racism, and racial capitalism. As revolutionary nationalists who linked political self-determination with anti-colonial thought; maverick socialists who talked of bringing Third World revolution to urban centers; and unconventional Marxists who expressed open admiration for Mao Zedong and Ho Chi Minh, the Black Panthers openly defied bourgeois liberal parameters of political engagement. The group fashioned itself as the vanguard of a political revolution capable of defending black lives from state-sanctioned violence, murder, and brutality. The Panthers called for an end to police brutality, the teaching of black history in schools, the end to capitalist exploitation that they linked to racial discrimination, and the release of African Americans from all local, state, and federal jails. But they were also grassroots activists who modeled radical self-love within communities, providing free school breakfasts, health clinics, legal aid, sickle-cell anemia testing, and busing to prisons to aid impoverished, racially segregated, and economically devastated black communities.

Johnson places reparations for slavery at the heart of his pursuit of racial justice. The Panthers did as well; it was in fact one of the group's deepest philosophical commitments. As keen students of history, they understood also that they were far from the first to demand this. As historian Mary Frances Berry illustrates in her biography of Callie House, the nineteenth-century leader of the National Ex-Slave Mutual Relief, Bounty, and Pension Association, the movement for reparations dates to the immediate aftermath of slavery. It was in fact a cause first championed by the formerly enslaved. House, whose organization represented about three hundred thousand freed slaves, fought an unsuccessful campaign to pass federal legislation that would have granted federal pensions to former slaves.

Calls for reparations have taken many different forms. Black Power activist James Foreman's "Black Manifesto" (1969) demanded that white churches and synagogues fund the creation of a half-billion-dollar trust that would be used for black infrastructure, including universities, publishing houses, legal aid, and farmland. The late-sixties Republic of New Afrika demanded the creation of a sovereign black country, carved out of the southern United States, as well as seed money of several billion dollars to sustain the new nation until it could be self-supporting. These utopian visions all share the goal of a viable black future, freed of the systemic disadvantages black Americans face, and which have their origins in slavery and its racial regime. They and their visionaries have been universally dismissed, ignored, mocked, reviled, and demonized by the mainstream, including often by black civil rights leaders. Johnson's embrace of the Movement for Black Lives' renewed call for reparations—like my own scholarship, which I have characterized as Black Power Studies—invites a reevaluation of how these historical visions of racial justice might offer clues to how the negative cycles of racial capitalism can be broken.

Often forgotten is that black studies—both in universities and in elementary, middle, and high schools—arose from midcentury radical efforts to overcome America's purposeful amnesia about black history and bring attention to the struggles of global people of color. Such efforts were enmeshed with calls for reparations: Foreman wanted black universities to be funded with reparations, and Black Power activists felt that quality education—formal or grassroots—was necessary if black people were to comprehend the full depth of their oppression and collectively demand recompense. Historian Russell Rickford's indispensable *We Are An African People* (2016) offers perhaps the definitive history of how black liberation movements used education to disrupt white supremacist institutions and epistemologies, and in the process attempted to practically implement Black Power's call for political self-determination through community control of institutions (and their finances) in American society.

Black Power, of course, both criticized liberal democratic capitalism and became partially commodified by it. And merely exposing racial capitalism's dark underbelly did not lead to its defeat. Arguably it is more entrenched now than ever. Nonetheless, in an era before Black Lives Matter offered an invigorating and timely assertion of black humanity and defense of black bodies, Black Power forged new ground by reimagining the very terms of debate between black people and the U.S. nation-state. Activists and organizers did so through bruising protests, massive urban revolts, organized demonstrations, school takeovers, boycotts, and civil disobedience. For example, historian Yohuru Williams's *Black Politics/ White Power* (2000) contextualizes the history of civil rights and Black Power in New Haven, Connecticut, by tracing the contours of how local civil rights activists paved the way for the Black Panthers to found one of the group's most important chapters, one that innovated the free breakfast programs and inspired protests at Yale University in 1970.

The Movement for Black Lives now continues this tradition, but updates it with a defiant recognition of black humanity in all of its messy, complex, and contradictory fullness. Youth, the elderly, the mentally and emotionally challenged, trans and queer, poor, the HIV-positive, and non-able-bodied are central to the radical democratic vision articulated in the Movement for Black Lives' "A Vision for Black Lives." In many ways, this agenda builds on earlier documents produced by the Black Liberation tradition: slave narratives, proceeds of Reconstruction-era Black Conventions, the anti-lynching journalism of Ida B. Wells, the Pan-African Congresses and their global black philosophies of Négritude and decolonization, and the Black Convention Movement of the 1960s and '70s, which featured Black Power conferences, the Congress of African Peoples Meeting, the Gary Convention, the African Liberation Support Committee, and the Sixth Pan-African Congress.

The legacy of Black Power informs Black Lives Matter in important and substantive ways, yet the contemporary movement has successfully overcome some of the former movement's conceptual shortcomings, especially with regard to its insistence that intersectionality is a strength of any social justice movement, rather than something to be denied, ignored, or silenced.

With its emphasis on the valor that ordinary people of color exhibit everyday just to survive in America, Black Lives Matter echoes the vision of no one more than it does that of Ella Baker. Baker, a tireless and instrumental crusader for civil rights who eschewed the spotlight because "strong people don't need strong leaders," found cause for hope in the fortitude and dreams of black citizens. Inspired by this, she shepherded the founding of SNCC, the most important grassroots organization of the era, one that catalyzed the 1960s and influenced the New Left, Black Power, the Black Panthers, and virtually every other radical organization since.

Baker eschewed hierarchies, personality cults, and iconography to get on with the work of liberation, a freedom she identified as offering ordinary people the chance to fashion their own dreams of empowerment, transformation, and dignity. She understood, better than perhaps any other black radical activist of the twentieth century, that humanity formed the beating heart of black liberation struggles, whether her fellow citizens recognized this or not.

This, Our Second Nadir
N. D. B. Connolly

IT HAS BEEN WORSE. Let's not forget "The Nadir," as the historian Rayford Logan coined it: the period following Reconstruction in which America witnessed the resurgence and bloody normalization of White Power politics. Between the 1870s and the turn of the twentieth century, southern whites took over the political and propaganda apparatus in all eleven states of the former Confederacy. They rewrote state constitutions with the explicit aim of disfranchising black voters. Racial terrorism, once held underground by the presence of federal troops, morphed into pogroms and spectacle lynchings carried out in broad daylight. Under piercing cries that "The South Will Rise Again," whites, sometimes by the hundreds and even thousands, attacked African Americans and their property. By some estimates, whites killed as many as half a million black people in politically motivated murders. These efforts were so terrifyingly effective that, over just one decade in Louisiana, white officials and vigilantes slashed the number of black registered voters from 130,000 to some 1,300—a decrease of 99 percent.

The Nadir coincided with the Gilded Age, and not by coincidence—a point Walter Johnson makes very clearly in his analysis of racial capitalism. As once-conquered Confederates snatched black people's legal protections, the courts and Congress elevated corporations to their current status as rights-bearing citizens. In their efforts to secure even modest concessions from capital, white workers abandoned and turned on black comrades, splintering interracial labor movements. "There began to rise in America in 1876," W. E. B. Du Bois remarked ruefully in *Black Reconstruction* (1935), "a new capitalism and a new enslavement of labor," one that bridled "white, yellow, brown and black labor." Then, as now, capitalism's malcontents, with their many colors, suffered a shared predicament. Fractured, "a living working class" transferred its "political power from the hands of labor to the hands of capital, where," Du Bois explained, "it has been concentrated ever since." In light of the ensuing imperialism, death, and evaporating livelihoods, the professor maintained, "God wept."

With the presidency of Donald Trump we can expect a Second Nadir. As was true during the first, white capital firmly holds the levers of both politics and propaganda. And if we expect to have any chance at all to prevent the losses of life and rights that white supremacy inevitably exacts, we are going to have to marshal a little Jim Crow wisdom—knowledge carried through and beyond the Nadir—about how racism got us into this mess.

The first lesson: we should expect steps back before we move forward. Liberal politicians will compromise with white supremacist, nativist, and chauvinist elements, this time in the Republican Party, further building inequality into the political system. The precedent is clear. In the forty years that followed mass black disfranchisement in the South, the best African Americans could hope for was the federalization of Jim Crow segregation. President Woodrow Wilson, a supposed reformer, expelled and demoted African Americans across the federal bureaucracy. From their safe congressional seats and with the power of the filibuster, southern congressmen and senators ensured that labor, housing, education, and hate crime legislation all favored southern designs, which included increased federal investment in sectors already controlled by capital—say, cotton cultivation—and minimal tampering with race regulations codifying Jim Crow.

The subsequent New Deal salvaged the American economy, in part by creating for mostly white employers, landlords, bankers, and developers a series of very profitable racial niche markets. Blocked from joining unions, blacks and agricultural workers, for instance, sold their labor for next to nothing, further protecting white wealth. Tenants in both rural and urban enclaves around the country—white and black—suffered gouging so dramatic that landlords could easily fetch annual returns of 25–60 percent on their rental investments. (Typical returns in white markets today stand at 4–6 percent.) These policies and others also set in motion another several decades of structured racial inequality as confined African American communities became sites of pointed, predatory taxation by white-controlled local governments and predatory pricing for durable goods, services, and housing.

Second lesson: in light of racist structures, we should not expect solidarity as the default response from subaltern people. In order to break out of Jim Crow regulations, many Americans elected to distance themselves from African Americans neighborhoods—sometimes violently—or simply denied, in spite of their African descent, being black altogether. In the century following the Nadir, people of all colors hungrily sought out political whiteness, either by passing for white or by pursuing legal or diplomatic exemptions from being "colored."

We should understand, though, that passing in the twenty-first century will not be of the kind depicted in black-and-white movies, for after the Second Reconstruction the meaning of whiteness changed. Everyone who could was suddenly in a hurry to disown it. Following the passage of the Civil Rights Act and the moral challenges of the broader black, brown, and red freedom struggles, scores of Americans bolted from whiteness looking to identify with any variation of "— American." Work by Matthew Frye Jacobsen, Nancy MacLean, Jared Sexton, and others explores how the hyphenated identities we now take as a given—and their "mixed race," "neither-black-nor-white" variants—emerged in the wake of Title VII of the Civil Rights Act. Affirmative action, new employment, and educational benefits were extended to those who could claim practically any association at all with the history of racial or ethnic discrimination in America. New forms of institutional multiculturalism in the 1960s and early 1970s distributed widely the government's obligation to redress historical wrongs. In place of so-called "Negro" benefits that could break down the vestiges of Jim Crow, practically everyone, in the eyes of the state, got to be some kind of minority.

This brings me to the third lesson: multiculturalism will not save us. Multiculturalism, as an alternative to mandated desegregation, is actually a southern—or, rather, segregationist—value, steeped in the elective traditions of southern liberalism. These include, in the Jeffersonian tradition, strict racial regulation and laissez-faire economics (the latter for whites only). Rather than mandated fair employment measures, decried by Jim Crow politicians as "autocratic" and "tyrannical," the country got affirmative action, a program that allows employers to cultivate their own multiculturalism relative to their own perceived market demands. Opposing the Court's decision in *Brown v. Board of Education* in 1954, Zora Neale Hurston argued against mandated integration with calls, instead, for "growth from within" and "ethical and cultural desegregation." This was a vision of culture over policy. Blacks and whites, her argument went, could come to understand each other on their own terms, not on terms set in some far-off bureaucracy in Washington.

As the 1960s became the 1970s—in battles over everything from school busing to anti-poverty measures—volunteerism and conflations of inequality with culture began to replace mandated desegregation efforts and an institutional acknowledgement of history. Indeed, white supremacy stays alive in American institutions through the pointed erasure of historical thinking, which is necessarily race thinking. The Supreme Court removed historical consciousness from college admissions policy in 1978 with its decision in *Regents of the University of California v. Bakke*; admissions committees could no longer consider past, group-based discrimination when determining individuals' present-day access to college. As Thurgood Marshall explained in his dissent, "It is more than a little ironic that, after several hundred years of class-based discrimination against Negroes, the Court is unwilling to hold that a class-based remedy for that discrimination is permissible." In its willful ahistoricism, the Court's rulings in *Bakke* and subsequent cases, including *Grutter v. Bollinger* (2003) and *Fisher v. University of Texas* (2013), have effectively affirmed a "diversity regime" that knows how to celebrate difference without exploring how that difference got produced, imposed, and preserved. The Court likewise removed historical consciousness from its federal voting rights protection in 2013 with *Shelby County v. Holder*, which ensured that states with a past record of racial discrimination no longer needed the presence of federal registrars at the polls. Representing what one observer viewed as the end of the Second Reconstruction, the *Shelby* decision opened the door for voter suppression in North Carolina and Florida in the 2016 election.

Contextualizing multiculturalism as one among many rejections of subaltern history thus reveals it to be, in large measure, just one more example of institutions behaving in observance of structural white preferences. The question is not whether to focus on culture, but rather which course of action advances institutional anti-racism as a collective aim.

Today calls to step away from "identity politics" represent implicit calls to step away from civil rights, as Marcus H. Johnson has powerfully argued. Such a move, again, merely represents an extension of older—indeed some of the oldest—segregationist politics. People often forget that *Plessy v. Ferguson* (1896), perhaps the most critical case in setting the terms for Jim Crow, professed to be a colorblind ruling. According to Justice Henry Billings Brown, segregation was not tantamount to discrimination. "We think the enforced segregation of the races," the Court said in a twisted logical turn, "neither abridges the privileges or immunities of the colored man, deprives him of his property without due process of the law, nor denies him the equal protection of the laws." No special treatment for black people, in other words, even as they suffered special indignities. Jim Crow's foundational ruling effectively stood on an "All Lives Matter" argument.

Now we are being asked to forget about race altogether. Even before Election Day wrapped up one of the most racist political campaigns in recent memory, white observers on the left, center, and right began telling us that what we had just witnessed was not about race. We were supposed to understand the hurting Heartland. Media outlets, reporters, and pundits, nursing their collective shock and groping for credibility, rolled out primitive "class vs. race" formulations. They warned the far left to "be careful with the 'white supremacy' label" and suggested that those who pursued "wrong-headed" "identity politics" owed middle America an apology.

But let's remember why Trump was able to surprise so many. One reason Trump seemed like such a long shot to liberals is that he failed to adhere to the general principles of the New Economy's dog-whistle race politics. The Second Reconstruction brought with it fundamental revisions in how America's political mainstream had to handle the race question. President Richard Nixon, mirroring approaches successfully deployed by Democratic mayors in Chicago and elsewhere, was forced to animate his party's white base not with overt calls to white racists, or even a successful Southern Strategy, but with calls for "law and order," full-throated defenses of "property rights," and condemnations of the "welfare ethic." These terms served as handy ways to target black populations, sometimes violently. Economic and federalist arguments could also be used to great effect. As the Republican strategist Lee Atwater explained in 1981, unaware he was being recorded:

> You start out in 1954 by saying, "Nigger, nigger, nigger." By 1968 you can't say "nigger"—that hurts you, backfires. So you say stuff like, uh, forced busing, states' rights, and all that stuff, and you're getting so abstract. Now, you're talking about cutting taxes, and all these things you're talking about are totally economic things and a byproduct of them is, blacks get hurt worse than whites. . . . "We want to cut this," is much more abstract than even the busing thing, uh, and a hell of a lot more abstract than "Nigger, nigger.". . . Anyway you look at it, race is going to be on the back burner.

Race on the back burner; economy, small government, and values on the front. The old, southern liberalism nationalized.

For about thirty years, tepid multiculturalism and other "colorblind" deployments of race and difference became the North Star for mainstream American politics. The charted course included civil rights organizations teaming up with corporations in the early 1980s to defend affirmative action against Ronald Reagan. Through the 1990s Bill Clinton's folksy, symbolic blackness (and the lingering white populism in the GOP) helped cement the Democratic Party's hold on the black vote, especially as it made "colorblind" policy overtures to white voters.

In response to the New Democrats, George W. Bush deployed an army of high-level black and brown surrogates and appointees to evidence the GOP's new "compassionate conservatism." And, of course, Barack Obama's *actual* blackness allowed him to openly scold his black base, to deport more than two million immigrants, all with little to no political cost. Following the Second Reconstruction, it seems, racial tolerance in general, and blackness in particular, became not just helpful but necessary for political success in America.

Then came Trump. Here was a man of questionable values, questionable conservative bona fides, and, based on his own checkered record in business, questionable understanding even of economics. Worse, it seemed, he again and again broke the discursive norms that had been greasing the wheels of American capitalism since the passage of the Civil Rights Act. Because Indiana-born judge Gonzalo Curiel was "a Mexican," Trump deemed him unqualified to adjudicate the Trump University fraud case. Because the NBC debate moderator Lester Holt was black, Trump decided he was a Democrat and thus part of the "phony system" propping up Hillary Clinton. (Holt is, in fact, a Republican.) Trump refused to be bound by the old Atwater playbook, and he won.

So, let's just tell the story right. Throughout the campaign Trump's base stood wealthier, not poorer, than the average voter who supported the Democrats. Exit polls showed that Clinton won more than half the votes of people who earn less than $50,000 a year. One-time Obama counties may have gone for Trump, but the mythical white millions who voted for Obama twice and then stomached a vote for Trump do not exist. The problem is rather that the two-time Obama voter—rather than vote for Clinton and, dare one say, pissed at the president himself—elected to stay home, especially if that voter was not college educated.

Which brings me to the final lesson: we need to practice our political consciousness. Class struggle requires a culture that nourishes class consciousness. Without cultural affirmations of feminism, attacks on women will not shock the conscience. The president-elect safely mocked the disabled, African Americans, and Latinos, performing his best in those areas where Americans enjoyed none of the intellectual and cultural infrastructure required to reject his brand of politics. On race specifically, our institutional priorities continue to undermine the formation of a racially literate public. You cannot topple racial injustice, sexism, or class exploitation without race, gender, or class thinking—early, often, and in public. And that requires, in place of mere "diversity," a restoration of historical thinking.

It also requires new protections of the electoral process. The American political system remains beholden to campaign contributions, corporate lobbying, and the slave masters' founding document, the Constitution. Every now and again we bend the system, in spite of its reluctance, into some temporarily progressive shape through legal challenges, grassroots community efforts, direct action, armed self-defense, and surreptitious subversions of everyday inhumanities. But remember: even as we try our damnedest (and we must), this will still take a while. It took nearly a century of work to achieve even the basic federal protections promised before the Nadir. Not until the March on Washington in 1963 would the country see another forceful show of solidarity between black civil rights groups and white organized labor. And not until the 1970s would African Americans reach the same number of elected or appointed officials nationwide that they once enjoyed in the South during Reconstruction.

It is uncertain when we will see our Third Reconstruction. I remain confident, though, that we will. We have been here before.

Racial Capitalism and Human Rights
Walter Johnson

> Are we not coming more and more, day by day, to making the statement
> 'I am white' the one fundamental tenet of our practical morality?
> —W. E. B. Du Bois, "The Souls of White Folk" (1920)

IN THEIR ERUDITION, imagination, and generosity, these essays provide ample evidence of the possibilities of political imagination beyond existing limits. So, I must begin by saying: Thank you.

The point of my essay—essay in the old-fashioned sense of "try"—was to attempt to recover a fuller notion of human emancipation, not to dispense with humanism as such. My premise is that a liberal account of human *rights*—of individual rights, of political rights, and even property rights—has come to dominate a broader humanist conversation about justice. Andrew Zimmerman points the way by quoting Aimé Césaire: "a true humanism—a humanism made to the measure of the world."

From Peter Linebaugh's incantory series "Am I Not a Man and a Brother?", "Ar'n't I a Woman?", and "I Am a Man"; to Manisha Sinha's invocation of African American abolitionists; to Peniel Joseph's reminder of the Nation of Islam's claim to be more fully human than whites, these essays map the coordinates of an intellectual history of humanism beyond liberalism: the black radical tradition.

Nor was my intention to simply dismiss liberal notions of justice or the long history of human rights, as invoked especially by Sinha but also by Roberto Gargarella. The better historian in my mind believes and wants to argue, along with Karl Marx, that liberal notions of justice, the rights of citizenship and human rights, are the summary moral achievements of the modern world. And yet: they provide only a foreshortened version of a thoroughgoing human emancipation. The fact that they have provided an indispensable resource for justice seekers of all sorts does not mean that we need to trim our imagination to the existing limits of the standing order. As Donna Murch argues, that order is all too quick to assert that the "identity" claims that emerge out of the history of settler colonialism are provincial hang-ups that stand in the way of liberal universalism.

I want to return to Murch's emphasis on U.S. settler colonialism, but I first need to finish the thread about human rights and "dehumanization." For better or worse, my argument was focused on the untheorized attribution of liberal, crypto-human-rights thinking to enslaved people: the collapse of "agency," liberalism, and the question of enslaved people's humanity into a tautological loop running endlessly through the historiography of slavery. Describing the actions of Nat Turner and Harriet Jacobs as equivalent episodes of the history of "agency," "freedom," or "human rights" is misleading. Indeed, doing so conscripts the history of slavery to a truncated version of the history of freedom (i.e., behind every resistance lies liberal agents expressing their full humanity and trying to regain their rights). In a longer project, I would have gone on to consider the ways anti-slavery frequently exceeded (or specified) the terms of liberal freedom, and then continued up through the history of the black radical humanism (and even the black liberal humanism) evident in so many of these responses.

Still, I think I would be critical of the notion that slavery "dehumanized" enslaved people. The ample usage of the terms "human," "man," and "woman" in anti-slavery texts does not in and of itself suggest that the terms of domination, exploitation, and resistance that characterized the daily lives of the enslaved were framed around the question of whether or not enslaved people were human beings. It might make good political sense to invoke a normative notion of humanity to critique injustice, whether or not one's own status as—or self-confidence in being—fully human has ever been threatened. And, even against the authority of Karl Marx by way of Grace Lee Boggs by way of Peter Linebaugh, I continue to think that we have more to lose by employing the word "dehumanization" than we have to gain from it. First, because it is sucked too easily into the culturally dominant notion of redress through human rights. Second, because it is too sticky: it leaves a trace of abjection on those it (sincerely) seeks to celebrate, advance, and protect. As Joseph puts it, it frames black history as a "never-ending audition" for humanity. I would rather begin with the way capitalism converts dead labor into living capital—transforming human beings through the simplification, instrumentalization, and eventual exhaustion of their capacity.

Along with Samuel Moyn, I would also still insist on a discontinuity between the inspiring historical profusion of black radical (and even liberal) humanism cited in these essays and the contemporary, culturally dominant notion of human-rights liberalism that my essay seeks to transcend. Notwithstanding the efforts of generations of black radicals to arraign the United States before the assembled authority of the United Nations, the efficacy of human rights claims has generally been outside the boundaries of the United States. Beyond the border: human rights, global justice, humanitarian intervention, and war crimes.

Within the border: "race relations," "law and order," capital punishment, mass incarceration, police violence, and impunity. The terrific breadth and variety of the black radical tradition as outlined in these pages represents a history and a political imaginary greatly in excess of human rights. It is precisely that discontinuity—the fact that the notion of human rights institutionalized in contemporary global governance does not descend from nor respond directly to the history of slavery, anti-slavery, and black radicalism more generally—that makes me want to insist that it should.

This historical discontinuity often causes quite diverse justice claims to be lumped together under the rubric of human rights. As Peter Hudson and Murch suggest, racial capitalist exploitation, white supremacist justification, and radical resistance take different shapes in different settings. Think of the different histories that underlie the struggles of our own recent past: the reparations claimed by the Movement for Black Lives; the (counter-)sovereignty defended by the Standing Rock Sioux; the sanctuary demanded by our undocumented neighbors. Each claim emerges out of and reflects, in mirror image, a specific history of economic exploitation, racial domination, and sexual invigilation: slavery, expropriation, casualization; Negro, Indian, Mexican; natal alienation; genocide and re-education; extraterritorialization; sexual vulnerability and violation in every case.

This sedimented history of racial capitalism in the United States, the "coproduction" of capitalist exploitation and racial domination, is exemplified in the essays by N. D. B. Connolly, Joseph, and Murch. And Hudson's admonition to think of the various aspects of the black radical tradition as arising out of "simultaneous, overlapping" circumstances —"not as mystical power, but as historical-material force"—helps explain why racism and capitalism must be understood as dialectically intertwined: the global operation of capital producing and depending upon differentiated and yet related racial formations all the world over.

Stephanie Smallwood captures the radical implications of this insight, reminding me of something I should have said. There is only dubious utility to any formal definition of capitalism that does not include the slave trade. So many of the most searching analyses of the slavery/capitalism question, including Caitlin Rosenthal's rich and informative piece, mobilize a host of modifiers—"pre-capitalism," "primary accumulation," "merchant capitalism," "war capitalism," etc.—to describe slavery as a variant form of capitalism while nevertheless maintaining some conceptual distance between the two. Smallwood turns the question around, insisting that we consider industrial capitalism to be a variant form of racial capitalism: a result of the history that began with the slave trade.

Connolly considers what these questions mean now that Donald Trump is president. As he suggests, much of the analysis in the aftermath of the election has been framed around an adventitious separation of the categories of "race" and "class": was Trump elected because of the economic anxieties of white people, or because of their racism? Recognizing the racial character of the neoliberal globalism that has undermined the security of much of the American working class—the fact that the global division of labor is also a racial and imperial division of labor—makes plain that the "economic anxiety" felt by many white Americans is ineluctably racial. The jobs they have lost have not simply disappeared: many of them have been relocated to places where labor has been exploited according to terms that are imperial and racial as well as simply economic. The immigrants they fear come not only in search of jobs, but in flight from social disorder created by the long history of U.S. imperial anti-communism and global neoliberal austerity.

As Du Bois wrote in *Black Reconstruction* (1935):

> Indeed, the plight of the white working class throughout the world today is directly traceable to Negro slavery in America, on which modern commerce and industry was founded, and which persisted to threaten free labor until it was partially overthrown in 1863. The resulting color caste founded and retained by capitalism was adopted, forwarded and approved by white labor, and resulted in subordination of colored labor to white profits the world over. Thus the majority of the world's laborers, by the insistence of white labor, became the basis of a system of industry which ruined democracy and showed its perfect fruit in World War and Depression.

Lamentably, Trump's success suggests that white—and especially white male—vulnerability is once again expressing itself as racial entitlement, rather than embracing the alternative path: away from fear and toward the more secure society for all offered by the black radical tradition. The once-again renounced covenant of Reconstruction and the promise of what Du Bois termed "abolition democracy" points us back to Marx: "Labor cannot emancipate itself in the white skin where in the Black it is branded."

Lake Michigan, Scene 22
Daniel Borzutzky

The dead man asks me where I want to fly

And I say I don't want to fly anywhere

I want to stay here and defend my people

And the dead man says who are your people

And I point to the list of the names of the missing people and I am clubbed over the head with a wooden oar and dragged away by the police to the overstuffed prison camp on the beach and I think that survival must be vulgar and I am taken to a coroner's office and there are tools on the cold metal table they lay me on and there are men in lab coats and there are attorneys and there is paperwork and they lay the paperwork over my body and someone comes to sign something and they sign the paper then a bureaucrat signs my leg and a nurse signs my leg and an attorney signs my leg and I come to understand that my leg is a legal document that will be filed in accordance with the necessary procedures needed to classify the remains of the dead

Outside the coroner's office the guard paces back in forth   inside I am the specimen

We are in a secret facility on the beaches of Lake Michigan   on the northern end of Chicago

This is where they take the bodies when they have finally stopped moving them from one holding cell to another

They move us from one police station to another until finally we are taken here as I have been taken here and tied to a burning radiator and my body burns and there are officers with guns pointing at my head asking me to confess to crimes I know nothing about and they turn the heat up on the radiator and I withstand the heat for a few more minutes but I cannot take the burn any longer and I tell them I am guilty

I tell them I have done the things they say I have done

I tell them I have committed crimes against humanity   murdered kidnapped   transported the bodies of small children from one part of the city to another

I am on the coroner's table and a priest comes in to offer me absolution and I tell him I don't want it because I am Jewish and they tell me I have no choice and the priest blesses my body so that I can leave the never-ending trauma of earth for the paradisiacal joy of heaven

Then they choke me until I die

And I am lying on the table dead and once more learning how to suffer

And I am lying with the other corpses and we are sick of being examined

We are sick of being identified

We are sick of being prodded and poked and groped and a man with a camera and notebook comes and says by way of explanation that this is only war

And for a second we are nothing at all and then we remember that once we were a strategical operation and we remember that once we were emblems of the state and we remember we have always been immigrants and we remember how they stoned us when we spoke our language and we remember the mobs of adolescents who stood over us   who spat on us and pissed on our faces and told us to never speak our words again

And the voice of the man who takes photos of our bodies says remember   this is only war

And another voice says   remember   this is only Chicago

And we are the corpses they stack on the beach

And we are the bodies that will be mauled by dogs and occupied by parasites

And we are the memory

And we are thousands of years old and they destroy us

They neutralize us

They execute us even though we are already dead

And they store us in a memorial that will open dozens of years from now   a memorial where they will display our beaten bodies to remind the future citizens of Chicago that this was only war and that forever we had always been dead

Borzutzky

Births of a Nation:
Surveying Trumpland with Cedric Robinson
Robin D. G. Kelley

CEDRIC ROBINSON WAS FOND of quoting his friend and colleague Otis Madison: "The purpose of racism is to control the behavior of white people, not Black people. For Blacks, guns and tanks are sufficient." Robinson used the quote as an epigraph for a chapter in *Forgeries of Memory and Meaning* (2007), titled, "In the Year 1915: D. W. Griffith and the Rewhitening of America." When people ask what I think Robinson would have said about the election of Donald Trump, I point to these texts as evidence that he had already given us a framework to make sense of this moment and its antecedents.

Robinson's work—especially his lesser-known essays on democracy, identity, fascism, film, and racial regimes—has a great deal to teach us about Trumpism's foundations, about democracy's endemic crises, about the racial formation of the white working class, and about the significance of resistance in determining the future.

> Through the intervention of film, a new American social order was naturalized.
> —Cedric J. Robinson

IN 1915 WILLIAM JOSEPH SIMMONS, an ex-preacher who made his income selling memberships in fraternal organizations, led a group of his friends atop Stone Mountain, just outside of Atlanta, burned a giant cross, and launched the revival of the Ku Klux Klan. His inspiration: seeing *The Birth of a Nation*, D. W. Griffith's three-hour paean to the original Klan. Simmons believed the new Klan could make America great again by purging it of un-American influences: Negroes, immigrants (except for those of Anglo and Scandinavian stock), Catholics, and Jews. Under the slogan "100 percent Americanism," the Klan pursued a program of severe immigration restriction, allegiance to the American flag, anti-communism, protecting white womanhood (and "correcting" wayward women who transgressed gender conformity, Protestant values, and the color line), better government, and law and order, while also engaging in lynching and open acts of terrorism against black people. The second Klan appears to be a ball of contradictions—antagonistic to both big business and industrial unions, contemptuous of both elites and a huge swath of the working class (the non-white and foreign-born). But as historian Sarah Haley recently argued, the Klan—whose membership rolls swelled to four million by 1924—mobilized a precarious middle class of small entrepreneurs, white-collar workers, and farmers facing the prospect of downward mobility and seeking hope in the elimination of the most marginalized segments of society.

In *Forgeries of Memory and Meaning*, Robinson explains why Griffith's film catalyzed this movement. This was no ordinary film. Based on Thomas Dixon's novel *The Clansman* (1905), it consolidated and circulated old racial fabulations and new fictions in the service of capitalist expansion and modern white supremacy—in the United States and abroad. *The Birth of a Nation* was historical alchemy, turning terrorists into saviors, rapists into chivalrous protectors of white women and racial purity, and courageous and visionary blacks into idle, irresponsible ignoramuses, rapists, and jezebels. Black people were not only unfit for democracy but they threatened social order. President Woodrow Wilson (who screened Griffith's film at the White House) praised it as American history written with lightning—and like lightning, its historical reworking had an obliterating effect on truth. Robinson identified it as a "rewhitening of America," a gallant effort to obliterate all vestiges of the black struggle for social democracy during Reconstruction.

For Robinson, 1915 marked the formation of a new "racial regime." With the term, Robinson meant:

> constructed social systems in which race is proposed as a justification for the relations of power. . . . [T]he covering conceit of a racial regime is a makeshift patchwork masquerading as memory and the immutable. Nevertheless, racial regimes do possess history, that is, discernible origins and mechanisms of assembly. But racial regimes are unrelentingly hostile to their exhibition. This antipathy exists because a discoverable history is incompatible with a racial regime . . . [and its] claims of naturalism.

Racial regimes, in other words, are fictions. As such, they are unstable, fragile, and contested. The scramble to prove black inferiority and buttress white racial democracy in the era of Jim Crow was no cakewalk. The previous era had unleashed the possibility of radical change in the United States, and that struggle continued well into the twentieth century, when armed insurrection, political assassination, lynching, disfranchisement, imperialism, and federal complicity in the triumph of white supremacy destroyed the last sigh of black-led biracial democratic, populist, and radical movements.

Robinson lays out in great detail all the sites of contestation in 1915, and all the operations the new racial regime masked in the process. He reminds us that Griffith's champion, Wilson, had opened the far Western Front of World War I when the United States invaded Haiti in 1915, long before the declaration of war on Germany. That intervention and long occupation (until 1934)—driven by U.S. finance capital—also required historical alchemy. The United States, the cause of much of Haiti's political and economic instability, had to see itself as the country's rescuing white knight. In the white American imagination, Haitians—like those blackface brutes in *The Birth of a Nation*—were seen as coons, niggers, and malevolent witchdoctors incapable of self-governance.

That May, W. E. B. Du Bois published "The African Roots of War" in *Atlantic Monthly*, a brilliant, prescient essay overshadowed by his folly three years later when he exhorted blacks to "close ranks" behind America's official entry into World War I. The essay not only reveals a global racial regime in which "the white workingman has been asked to share the spoil of exploiting 'chinks and niggers,'" but argues that we will never rid the world of war nor achieve democracy until we eradicate racism and colonialism. And who could lead the struggle to topple this rapacious system? None other than the descendants of "the European slave trade . . . the ten million black folk of the United States, now a problem, then a world salvation."

The stage was set: D. W. Griffith's New Nation versus the New Negroes. The latter resisted with pickets and boycotts, speeches and editorials, scholarship and art, and outright rebellion. They exposed the racial regime for what it was, the tyranny of white supremacy masquerading as enlightened democracy. The former, backed by finance capital and the academy, manufactured the Negro as Problem, a campaign accelerated through newer technologies of mass media. Film—whether newsreel footage of U.S. Marines entering Port-au-Prince or Griffith's robed Klansmen saving the virginal Elsie Stoneman from the clutches of a rapacious mulatto—can mask and reorder social reality, turning victims into perpetrators and transforming imperialism into a rescue operation.

Robinson demonstrates that the post-Reconstruction order was not a return to the antebellum but a new racial and economic order that deployed a reinvention of the past in the service of a new regime. If new media played a key role, print was also crucial to this campaign. In 1916 *The Passing of the Great Race*, eugenicist Madison Grant's chilling case for racial cleansing, became a national bestseller. Adolf Hitler praised the book as foundational to his own thinking. Grant's book had plenty of company in the decade, including Robert W. Shufeldt's *America's Greatest Problem: The Negro* (1915) and Lothrop Stoddard's *The Rising Tide of Color Against White World Supremacy* (1920). White supremacy traverses the ideological spectrum, even now. Many foundational texts of the Progressive Era's racial regime were penned by liberal social scientists obsessed with the challenges of race and empire for American democracy. Many shared the eugenicists' presumption that democracy's survival depends on the suppression of difference.

Franklin H. Giddings, in his 1901 book *Democracy and Empire*, coined the phrase "democratic empire" to suggest that imperial expansion was itself a democratizing project. It was more than just the introduction of modern infrastructure, Western education, and civilization. It was the creation of social cohesion through the rapid assimilation of subject peoples. Giddings insisted that social cohesion or some sense of solidarity is a precondition of democracy, and racial difference renders such solidarity improbable if not impossible. Sociologist John Moffatt

Mecklin, a self-proclaimed Progressive liberal, published *Democracy and Race Friction: A Study in Social Ethics* the year before the release of *The Birth of a Nation*. He argues that racism and discrimination undermine democracy, but at the same time puts much of the blame on the cultural differences and "hereditary instincts" of non-whites (e.g., weak powers of inhibition, criminality, inability to control sexual impulses). Thus, while recognizing racism as a fetter on democracy, he nonetheless apologizes for white supremacy, arguing that blacks and whites have very different value systems. White supremacy is therefore a "form of self-preservation." (He is silent on whether lynching and rape were "moral" elements of self-preservation.) The solution? Mecklin believed "industrial competition" will allow the laws of natural selection to determine the fate of non-whites, producing the "ethnic homogeneity" necessary for "an efficient democracy."

While these texts were influential, Griffith's masterwork and films that followed in its wake proved indispensable for installing the modern racial regime. The consequences, however fragile, were devastating—not just for African Americans but for working-class whites. As Robinson writes, Griffith and this emergent film industry

> constituted the social and cultural platform for a robust economic and political agenda; an agenda in the process of seizing domestic and international labor, land, and capital. . . . White patrimony deceived some of the majority of Americans, patriotism and nationalism others, but the more fugitive reality was the theft they themselves endured and the voracious expropriation of others they facilitated. The scrap which was their reward was the installation of Black inferiority into their shared national culture. It was a paltry dividend, but it still serves.

I love the poorly educated.
—Donald J. Trump

THE DIVIDEND STILL SERVES. Many who voted for him, including those of the alt-right, flocked to Trump because he villainized immigrants, black people, and anti-patriotic business moguls who sent jobs overseas. Most pundits insist that Trump appeals not to white racism but to working-class populism driven by class anger. If this were true, why didn't Trump win over droves of black and brown voters, since they make up the lowest rungs of the working class and suffered disproportionately more than whites during the financial crisis of 2008? Instead Trump's victory inspired a wave of racist attacks and emboldened white nationalists to flaunt their allegiance to the president-elect.

The response on the part of high-profile liberals and leftists has been to blame "identity politics" for undermining the potential for working-class solidarity. Mark Lilla's *New York Times* screed, "The End of Identity Liberalism," is a case in point. "In recent years," writes Lilla, "American liberalism has slipped into a kind of moral panic about racial, gender and sexual identity that has distorted liberalism's message and prevented it from becoming a unifying force capable of governing." The result is a "generation of liberals and progressives narcissistically unaware of conditions outside their self-defined groups, and indifferent to the task of reaching out to Americans in every walk of life." In other words, people of color, queer folks, feminist-minded women, and liberal Democrats alienated the white working class, driving it into the arms of Trump.

The argument is both inept and confused. The movements associated with "identity liberalism" have not been obsessed with narrow group identities but with forms of oppression, exclusion, and marginalization.

And these movements are not exclusionary—not Black Lives Matter, not prison abolitionists, not movements for LGBTQ, immigrant, Muslim, and reproductive rights. They are serious efforts to interrogate the sources of persistent inequality, the barriers to equal opportunity, and the structures and policies that do harm to some groups at the expense of others.

Of course, Lilla's arguments are hardly new. At the height of the culture wars, conservatives such as Gertrude Himmelfarb, William Bennett, and Lynne Cheney; liberals such as Arthur Schlesinger and Allan Bloom; and self-styled leftists such as Todd Gitlin and Michael Tomasky argued that identity politics had undermined a unified America founded on Enlightenment principles of individualism, liberty, and secularism. A number of pundits have called Richard Rorty's *Achieving Our Country* (1998) prophetic because it warns that continued downward mobility of the white working class and growing income inequality would lead to the rise of a strongman with authoritarian tendencies. Rorty's thesis was not a critique of neoliberal policies, however, but a critique of the academic left and its love affair with identity politics. "Nobody is setting up a program in unemployed studies, homeless studies, or trailer-park studies," Rorty laments, "because the unemployed, the homeless, and the residents of trailer parks are not 'other' in the relevant sense." Anyone who works on these issues at the university—then and now—will find Rorty's assertion laughable.

Rorty, a brilliant philosopher with genuine concern for working people, nevertheless mistook *ideology*—a categorical opposition to racism, sexism, homophobia, institutional oppression, and marginalization based on difference—for "identity politics," while presuming that the white working class is operating purely out of race- and gender-neutral economic interests.

More conservative critics of identity politics sought to rescue Western culture from its anti-racist, feminist, and post-colonial critics.

In his famous attack on multiculturalism, Arthur Schlesinger writes, "it was the West, not the non-Western cultures, that launched the crusade to abolish slavery.... Those many brave and humane Africans who are struggling these days for decent societies are animated by Western, not by African, ideals. White guilt can be pushed too far." So far, in fact, that "political correctness" has been perceived as an attack on intellectual freedom and American virtues.

Robinson likened such antinomies to Christian attacks on heresy during the Middle Ages. In a short essay titled "Multiculturalism and Manichaeism," he acknowledges what many critics of so-called "political correctness" understood: that the Schlesingers and Blooms and their compatriots across the ideological spectrum are holding on to "an imaginary transcendent universal culture—the West," a nostalgia for a university that never was, and a mythic American identity presumably forged through an enlightened process of deracination. But Robinson knew there was more at stake. "They wish to erase the exposed seam," he writes, "the nexus between power and regimes of knowledge so forcefully articulated by Michel Foucault. How else can one defend their specious histories of knowledge, which invoke some pristine mythical moment in the life of the American academy?"

This is not to say that Robinson's defense of multiculturalist discourse was uncritical. He pointed to the dangers of an essentialism that reduces complex, historical experiences to fixed, discrete racial, ethnic, and gender identities. And to the left's claim that Marxism is our way out of the Manichean world of fixed difference versus false universalism, Robinson politely demurred, citing arguments he made in *Black Marxism* a decade earlier. What he proposes instead is

> that a radical impulse in multiculturalism constitutes both a critique of the absences and an appropriation of the positive contributions of Marx-

ism. We are not the subjects or the subject formations of the capitalist world-system. It is merely one condition of our being.... Multiculturalism, then, is a site of discursive resistance, and emblem of articulation of several trajectories of 'objective' opposition (religious, nationalist, feminist, etc.) mounted by our peoples in the everyday world.

Democratic philosophy was subverted by plutocracy ... whose rulers depended on the preservation of a slave economy, the exploitation of 'white' laborers (male and female), the severe restriction of women's political rights, and the expropriation of Native Americans.
—Cedric J. Robinson

OPPONENTS OF TRUMPISM—and what it portends for the future of our democratic system—are scrambling to find both "the seed of opposition" and the roots of the crisis. Locating the elusive seed of opposition is a daunting task, but it seems that most people agree that repairing our broken democracy ought to be our priority.

Cedric Robinson had a lot to say about democracy—as a theory, an aspiration, and a fiction. As a child of World War II who came of age with the Cold War and the civil rights movement, he encountered the word "democracy" at every turn. Democracy was bandied about as an explanation for America's frequent military excursions abroad, while at home it was an elusive dream for which black people were arrested, beaten, even killed.

Robinson studied democracy at the University of California, Berkeley, and fought for it as a leader of the campus NAACP and as an activist in SLATE, a forerunner of the Berkeley Free Speech Movement. In the summer of 1962, he witnessed firsthand a struggle to create a multiethnic democracy in Southern Rhodesia crushed by the state. He was there under the auspices of Operation Crossroads—a precursor to the Peace Corps that sent student volunteers to Africa to help build libraries, schools, and community centers. Founded by Harlem Presbyterian minister James H. Robinson and backed by the Rockefeller Brothers Fund, Operation Crossroads was also a Cold War project designed to combat communism and spread American democracy to the continent. During his month-long stay, Cedric watched the U.S.-backed regime led by the fascist Rhodesian Front violently repress and ultimately outlaw the Zimbabwe African People's Union (ZAPU). Upon his return to Berkeley, Robinson enrolled in three political science courses, including one on African politics, in his quest to comprehend democracy, and he would go on to do graduate work in political science at San Francisco State University and at Stanford.

In an essay titled "African Politics: Progression or Regression?" written for a Stanford graduate seminar taught by David Abernethy (then a young scholar who wrote on popular education in Africa), Robinson argued that the newly "decolonized" territories in Africa were *not yet* nations. For him the "birth" of decolonialized African states required shedding Western political structures and creating their own political institutions. More provocatively, he suggests that the modern nation-state is, in fact, "a regression or step backward from the stateless societies of some earlier African history." Here he begins to reveal the seeds of his argument in *Black Marxism* (1983) that the black petit bourgeoisie was disconnected from the political and cultural traditions that sustained anti-colonial movements in the past. He writes that those living in exile or European educated "have betrayed the heritage of their predecessors in the 19th and early 20th centuries," indigenous leaders "who were committed through their own particular missions to the recovery of life with integrity for the mass of African people." The alternative path he imagines is not based on modernization theory or industrialization but something different:

> Perhaps what is needed are new political organisations without single or even multiple leaders, but with no leaders at all. . . . That is a sophisticated social organization; a primitive organization is one where the courts are filled with defendants bound and gagged or where its citizens must be shot down in the streets and terrorized in to fitful conformity.

Robinson never abandoned this radical utopian vision of democracy, although as the promise of the 1960s and '70s faded into the revanchism of the 1980s and '90s, he turned to the genesis of the "primitive organization" that became the U.S. political system. He traced the ideological roots of U.S. democracy back to the profoundly anti-democratic strain in Plato and Aristotle. For Robinson the "crisis" of democracy was not simply the result of the corrosive forces of neoliberalism but endemic from its very inception. His provocative essay "Slavery and the Platonic Origins of Anti-Democracy" (1995) locates the genesis of anti-democracy in *The Republic*, which accepts slavery and proposes a theory of enlightened governance that excludes the popular classes. Slavery in Plato's politics was an immutable fact, the slave an inferior being bereft of reason and thus incapable of participating in democracy, let alone governing. "Plato's political theory," writes Robinson, "thus repressed the history of popular rebellion and with it the recognition that social agency might have its genesis from the general populace. Even in his 'treatment' of the degeneracy of democracy to tyranny, the demos is denied true agency through the selection of a demagogue." Robinson wryly concludes, "In its antidemocratic plutocratic prejudice, the Republic provides an authority rich in intellectual strategems *a propos* to the political discourse embedded in the American political order. Plato survives because if he had not existed, he would have to be invented."

It should come as no surprise that the founding fathers were avid readers of Plato and Aristotle, who were—along with Homer—the pillars of classical philosophy in the eighteenth and nineteenth centuries. Distrust of democracy was widespread. James Madison even positively described the new state as an "oligarchy." Landholding, Madison insisted, had to be a requirement for participation in the body politic "as to protect the minority of the opulent against the majority." The result, besides property requirements for voting, was the Electoral College. For some proponents, the Electoral College would be the enlightened check against the threat of an ignorant populace backing a demagogue as president. But it also guaranteed a pro-slavery White House. Basic to the college's architecture was the Three-Fifths Compromise, the rule that congressional representation in the slave states would be apportioned by counting the white population along with 60 percent of enslaved people. The number of electors was to be equal to the number of representatives and senators from each state. This gave the slaveholding South an edge in presidential elections compared to other states, and that advantage lasted well after slavery ended, since the vast majority of black southerners were disfranchised after Reconstruction.

Ironically, critics of the Electoral College who believe Hillary Clinton should be president based on the popular vote are now invoking Alexander Hamilton's idea of the "conscientious" elector who will buck party affiliation in order to make the enlightened choice. Hence, an anti-democratic institution is invoked as both the problem and solution, fueling the myth of American democracy's singular genius while remaining "openly hostile to the periodic outbreaks of what it redundantly terms 'participatory' or 'direct' democracy."

> When the performance of charismatic leadership stands in for building movements and relationships, for grassroots political education, and for a practiced commitment to disassembling social hierarchies, the promise of social justice and political empowerment is endangered by a formation of authority that limits our capacities to remake the world.
> —Erica R. Edwards

IN 2016, ON THE HEELS of the centennial celebration of D. W. Griffith's *The Birth of a Nation*, the Sundance Film Festival screened a new film bearing the same title. Nate Parker, the young African American actor who wrote, directed, and starred in the film appropriated the title from Griffith as a deliberate provocation. His historical epic is about Nat Turner, the Virginia slave-turned-minister who led the bloodiest slave revolt in U.S. history. Like Griffith, Parker simultaneously revised history while reflecting and refracting current political realities. It is impossible to watch Parker's *The Birth of a Nation* without recalling the recent wave of police killings and rage and resistance it has generated. Yet whereas Griffith's racist epic made history, Parker's film flopped. Revelations of Parker's involvement in a sexual assault twenty years earlier dampened ticket sales, and cinematic representations of black rebellion tend to do poorly at the box office. But neither adequately explains the film's epic failure.

In both *Birth*s, women are territory to be fought over, attacked, and defended. Whereas the Klan avenged the nation and their manhood by rooting out alleged black rapists, Turner and his men avenged *their* nation and *their* manhood for the rape of their women by white masters and overseers. As critic and historian Salamishah Tillett observed, Parker's film thus silences black women, turning them into mute victims.

"In denying these women their revolutionary gestures, Mr. Parker risks making them objects that he, and only he, can freely move around the screen." Noting the film's appearance during the height of black resistance to police violence, she adds that its emphasis on the male charismatic leader is "out of step" with the Movement for Black Lives and its largely black female leadership. I would add that the movement's embrace of black queer feminism, its horizontal leadership model, and emphasis on deliberative, participatory democracy counter the film's central vision.

Robinson understood the charismatic figure in insurgent movements as "the expression of a people focused onto one of their members . . . the responsive instrument of a people," rather than the force or agent directing the people forward. This is certainly not how Parker portrayed Turner, which suggests that Robinson may have been sympathetic to Tillet's reading of the film. But he would have also insisted that the female-led, horizontal formations resisting state violence today are not aberrations but consistent with the black radical tradition. H. L. T. Quan reminds us of the centrality women in Robinson's historical archeology of black revolt. "Indeed," Quan writes, "the women who people Robinson's imagination are not the anorexic two-dimensional (mainstream) feminist heroines whom we often encounter in gender-related texts, but the plotters of history. They are women of substance, of imagination, of formidable social force, women who would kill and wage revolutions against the state and the world economy."

Just as Nat Turner's rebellion portended chattel slavery's violent demise, today's organized protests in the streets and other places of public assembly portend the rise of a police state in the United States. For the past five years, the insurgencies of the Movement for Black Lives and its dozens of allied organizations have warned the country that unless we end racist state-sanctioned violence and the mass caging of black and brown people, we are headed for a fascist state.

Others argue that fascism is already here. Refusing to play politics, they criticize both Democrats and Republicans. They have angered cops by insisting that no law officer is above reproach. Skeptical of courtroom justice, they have taken to the streets, social media, the press, and even the United Nations, placing the moral, ethical, and legal question about the value of black lives before the world court of opinion. The movement has also proposed a plan to divest from a society of punishment, inequality, environmental degradation, and white supremacy and invest in a future built on free education, healthcare, housing, living-wage jobs, decriminalization, restorative justice in lieu of caging, food justice, and green energy. We need to remember this before more angry liberals—forgetting the misogynist strain in white identity politics—blame the Movement for Black Lives for Clinton's defeat and for mau-mauing white folks into the arms of Trump.

Those of us who lived through the Reagan era have seen these dynamics before, though on a smaller scale. Ronald Reagan's election not only owed much to white working-class resentment and middle-class white homeowners seeking tax relief, but his ascent to office coincided with heightened police and vigilante violence. In 1979 in Greensboro, North Carolina, the Ku Klux Klan assassinated five members of the Communist Workers Party in broad daylight. In Mississippi in 1980, at least twelve African Americans were lynched. The same year at least forty racially motivated murders occurred in cities as diverse as Buffalo, Atlanta, and Mobile. Across the country, police killings and non-lethal acts of brutality generated protests, notably a massive urban rebellion in Liberty City, Florida. And during Reagan's eight years in office, the number of hate crimes reported annually in the United States grew threefold. Faced with a dramatic rise in racism, unemployment, and homelessness, followed by deep cuts in social programs and increases in military spending, black resistance ramped up. The late historian and activist Manning Marable had even referred to 1980 as "The Red Year," a revolutionary moment similar to 1919.

Robinson shared some of Marable's optimism. It was, after all, the period in which he wrote *Black Marxism*, which compelled him to undertake a substantive study of fascism since the book's three main subjects—W. E. B. Du Bois, C. L. R. James, and Richard Wright—were all radicalized during the 1930s. The dark times under Reagan resonated with his reading of the history of America's support of fascism. For example, the American capitalist class was sympathetic to Benito Mussolini's fascist regime. J. P. Morgan loaned Italy in excess of $100 million in 1926, and *Fortune Magazine*, the *Saturday Evening Post*, *Business Weekly*, and the *New Republic* all ran admiring spreads on Italian fascism up until the mid-1930s. Robinson's central point was that the black masses not only *anticipated* the rise of fascism, they resisted before it was considered a crisis. Robinson called them "premature antifascists," noting that they had stood in stark opposition to those elites enamored with fascism, "which gave primacy to the interests of the State as an instrument of racial 'destiny.'"

Trump's election does *not* signal the strengthening and consolidation of U.S. power but its decline. Contemporary resistance movements did not ensure Clinton's defeat, but they did reveal the regime's fragility. The Movement for Black Lives, Black Lives Mater, the Dream Defenders, Black Youth Project 100, We Charge Genocide, Million Hoodies, the Moral Mondays Movement, the uprisings in Baltimore and Ferguson—not to mention the immigrant rights movement, and the ongoing struggle in Standing Rock in defense of Native sovereignty and against the war on the planet—all presaged and accelerated the current crisis of the state.

Robinson teaches us that racial regimes are unstable. They can be disassembled, though that is easier said than done. In the meantime, we need to be prepared to fight for our collective lives. I can hear Cedric's timely counsel in the aftermath of George W. Bush's "fraudulent" defeat of Al Gore in 2000: "For the moment . . . an unelected government has seized illegal powers. That must be opposed with every democratic weapon in our arsenal."

From *Good Stock / Strange Blood*
Dawn Lundy Martin

> *Symptomatic of being a slave is to forget you're a slave, to participate in industry as a critical piece in its motor. At night you fall off the wagon because it's like falling into your self.*

—fetish object—

deploy sensory mechanism

deploy sound canon

blow their fucking eardrums out

shoot them at close range if you can

rationale of the uninterrogated actual

in the sideyard bright wind takes up sprinkler's sprinkles into sunlight

Formulations—

      that you can discover anywhere. In the Mayan ruins, you find a remnant: dust it off, take the sheath off, reveal it to known world and say, *here is the world before*. What do we know from this fragile dust, we ask? We are a civilization who knows civilization. The feeling itself comes from this tiny ignorance. Call it a blind spot. Call it a shoe worn over whole magics. You wander into a space that smells of the love of your life sprinkling lavender onto your chest. You inhale so deeply you have to spit. To love incessantly despite the reader's inability to extract anything at all from the remnant. *We can already look back*, says the reader. The worn-down stone at your toe. The ate-up nachos from yesterday. They will say they are not from yesterday but it's true. They are. The nachos shat out in the toilet. The toilet barely flushing. And, how's a man to strut? How's a strut to cock-hand, walking *oe'r the land of the free*, the weeping feet. A mother lost, a singer dead. The words "we hope." The abstractions of "strength" and "virtue." They have it in the song. We sang the song eerie she interrupted the song barely unable to hear it sung. The land. The brave. The destitute. I worry. But, no space for endings. We could bury ourselves here. Or not. Or not.

Further Reading

In addition to the work of our contributors, the editors recommend:

Banner, Stuart. *How the Indians Lost Their Land: Law and Power on the Frontier* (Cambridge, MA: Harvard University Press, 2005).

Boggs, Grace Lee, and James Boggs. *Revolution and Evolution in the Twentieth Century* (New York: Monthly Review Press, 1974).

Davis, Angela. *The Meaning of Freedom: And Other Difficult Dialogues* (San Francisco: City Lights, 2011).

Du Bois, W. E. B. *Black Reconstruction in America* (1935).

———. "The Souls of White Folk" (1920).

Haley, Sarah. *No Mercy Here: Gender, Punishment, and the Making of Jim Crow Modernity* (Chapel Hill: UNC Press, 2016).

Hall, Stuart, et al. *Policing the Crisis: Mugging, the State, and Law and Order* (London: Macmillan, 1978).

James, C. L. R. *The Black Jacobins: Toussaint L'Ouverture and the San Domingo Revolution* (1938).

Lipsitz, George. *The Possessive Investment in Whiteness: How White People Profit from Identity Politics*, rev. ed. (Philadelphia: Temple University Press, 2006).

Lowe, Lisa. *The Intimacies of Four Continents* (Durham: Duke University Press, 2015).

Marx, Karl. *Capital* (1867).

Montoya, María E. *Translating Property: The Maxwell Land Grant and the Conflict over Land in the American West, 1840–1900 (Berkeley: University of California Press, 2002).

Morgan, Jennifer. *Laboring Women: Reproduction and Gender in New World Slavery* (Philadelphia: University of Pennsylvania Press, 2004).

Painter, Nell Irvin. *The History of White People* (New York: W. W. Norton, 2010).

Robinson, Cedric J. *Black Marxism* (Chapel Hill: UNC Press, 1983).

———. *Black Movements in America* (New York: Routledge, 1997).

———. *Forgeries of Memory and Meaning: Blacks and the Regimes of Race in American Theater and Film before World War II* (Chapel Hill: UNC Press, 2007).

Rodney, Walter. *How Europe Underdeveloped Africa* (Washington: Howard University Press, 1974).

Saunt, Claudio. *A New Order of Things: Property, Power, and the Transformation of the Creek Indians, 1733–1816* (Cambridge, UK: Cambridge University Press, 1999).

Saxton, Alexander. *The Rise and Fall of the White Republic: Class Politics and Mass Culture in Nineteenth-Century America* (New York: Verso, 1990).

White, Richard. *The Middle Ground: Indians, Empires, and Republics in the Great Lakes Region, 1650–1815* (Cambridge, UK: Cambridge University Press, 2010).

Williams, Eric. *Capitalism and Slavery* (1944).

Contributors

Dwayne Betts is a poet, memoirist, and teacher. His most recent book is *Bastards of the Reagan Era*.

Daniel Borzutzky is a Chilean-American translator and poet. His most recent book, *The Performance of Becoming Human*, won the 2016 National Book Award in Poetry.

N. D. B. Connolly is Herbert Baxter Adams Associate Professor of History at Johns Hopkins University and author of *A World More Concrete: Real Estate and the Remaking of Jim Crow South Florida*.

Roberto Gargarella is Professor of Constitutional Theory at the Universidad de Buenos Aires and researcher at Argentina's National Scientific and Technical Research Council.

Peter James Hudson is Assistant Professor of History and African American Studies at UCLA. His first book, *Bankers and Empire: How Wall Street Colonized the Caribbean*, is forthcoming from University of Chicago Press.

Walter Johnson, Winthrop Professor of History and of African and African American Studies at Harvard University, directs the Charles Warren Center for Studies in American History. He is author of *Soul by Soul* and *River of Dark Dreams: Slavery and Empire in the Cotton Kingdom*.

Peniel Joseph, Professor of Public Affairs at the University of Texas, Austin, was the founding director of the Center for the Study of Race and Democracy at Tufts University. He is author of *Stokely: A Life*.

Robin D. G. Kelley, Gary B. Nash Professor of American History at UCLA, is author of *Africa Speaks, America Answers: Modern Jazz in Revolutionary Times* and *Freedom Dreams: The Black Radical Imagination*.

Peter Linebaugh is an historian. Among other books he is author of *The London Hanged*. His forthcoming study of the commons is called *Ned & Kate: A Love Story among the Atlantic Mountains*.

Dawn Lundy Martin is a poet, member of the Black Tool Collective, and co-founder of the Third Wave Foundation. Her most recent book is *Life in a Box Is a Pretty Life*.

Samuel Moyn is Jeremiah Smith, Jr. Professor of Law and History at Harvard University and author, most recently, of *Christian Human Rights*.

Donna Murch is Associate Professor of History at Rutgers University and author of *Living for the City: Migration, Education, and the Rise of the Black Panther Party in Oakland, California*.

Caitlin Rosenthal is Assistant Professor of History at the University of California, Berkeley. Her first book, *From Slavery to Scientific Management*, is forthcoming from Harvard University Press.

Manisha Sinha, Professor of Afro-American Studies and Adjunct Professor of History at the University of Massachusetts, Amherst, is author of *The Slave's Cause: A History of Abolition*.

Stephanie Smallwood is Associate Professor of History at the University of Washington and author of *Saltwater Slavery: A Middle Passage from Africa to American Diaspora*.

Andrew Zimmerman, Professor of History and International Affairs at George Washington University, is author, most recently, of *Alabama in Africa: Booker T. Washington, the German Empire, and the Globalization of the New South*.